DON'T TELL ME

A Journey from Farm Girl to CEO

SANDRA JAMES

DON'T TELL ME I CAN'T

A Journey from Farm Girl to CEO

Cover photography by Garage 26.

Don't Tell Me I Can't/Sandra James. -- 1st ed.

ISBN: 978-1-990830-62-4

This book is dedicated to my sons, Adam James and Cole James, and my husband Martín Del Carmen, the loves of my life.

"The first step towards getting somewhere is to decide you're not going to stay where you are."

—J.P. Morgan

"Change, by its very nature, is threatening but it is also often productive."

—Betty Ford

Change your attitude,
Change your mind,
Change your life.

A quote on a card I carried in my wallet
for three decades after getting sober.

Revenue is vanity; profit is sanity!

—Sandra James

I learned this about business the hard way.

Table of Contents

Preface

Have you ever…

Been scared?

Been abused?

Been addicted to drugs or alcohol?

Been homeless?

Been told you can't do something?

Gotten divorced?

Been a single mother?

Been an entrepreneur?

Had someone you loved die?

Failed and started again?

If you have, this book is for you.

I hope it brings you inspiration and hope for what is possible.

Never give up!

Is This All God's Got In-Store for Me?

On July 4, 1988, I hit rock bottom. My friend, Lisa, and I were celebrating the holiday in San Diego, and it was a beautiful, sunny Southern California day. Only I didn't feel beautiful or sunny as Lisa drove us down the freeway in her white Toyota Supra. Lisa and I were friends who did drugs together and I was begging her to share her cocaine to help me feel better. I was working on achieving "clean and sober" but had relapsed many times. Knowing that I became paranoid when I did drugs, Lisa wouldn't give me anything, not because she wanted me to be clean, but because she was afraid, I would jump out of the moving car and kill myself.

"We're on the San Diego Freeway, Lisa," I said. "You really think I would do that?"

"I think it's a serious possibility," she replied, with a sideways glance at me. "You are no fun high anymore."

I was stunned. Who was she to withhold drugs? She and I had been partying together for years and we always shared. I felt indignant and defensive. Damnit, *I was fun*! Yet…. I also wondered, how I had sunk so low in my addiction to cocaine that my *drug friend* was afraid I was going to kill myself?

Later, when we were partying at a club, I finally convinced Lisa to share her cocaine with me. Within a half hour, a sickening paranoia enveloped me while I was in the women's restroom, and I wondered, was this all God had in store for me?

One never knows when or where God will speak to you, but I never imagined God would talk to me in the women's restroom at a nightclub. I took a quick inventory of where I was in life and there was nothing appealing about it. My drug dealer boyfriend, who was my source for both drugs and money, ghosted me. I learned that even though he was divorced he had returned to his ex-wife and two kids. I'd had to sell the beautiful Z28 Camaro he bought me and the car I'd replaced it with was repossessed. I was reduced to walking everywhere in the Phoenix summer heat.

I had been using cocaine and vodka like an on/off switch every day. Any future plans I entertained centered on securing the next high. I currently had to beg, borrow -- and sometimes worse -- to afford the addictions that I thought were essential to my hopeless life.

Maya Angelou wrote, "The need for change bulldozed a road down the center of my mind." I had an epiphany in that restroom: either I needed to change my life or go ahead and leap out of a moving car next time we were on the San Diego Freeway.

I decided to change my life.

Less than three years later, I made my first million dollars.

———◆◆———

Thanks for the Work Ethic

I grew up on various farms that my dad tried to make work. Educated as an engineer, Dad loved farming and he worked to make the farms feed and clothe our large family. After he served in the U.S. Air Force, he and my mother bought a farm in Torrington, Wyoming, and tried to make it successful.

Dad was a cowboy, always in Wrangler jeans, button-down shirts, boots and a hat to cover his bald head. Standing only 5 feet, 10 inches at most, he was a tough man who pounded a strict work ethic in each of us, whether we wanted it or not. His dream of having a family of all boys who would help him on the farm was crushed when there was only one male in the first six kids. He made do with what he had, putting us to work almost as soon as we could walk. Four years later, he had another son. Over the next decade he added another son and another daughter, enlarging our family to just one short of a dozen.

A few years after declaring bankruptcy on the farm in Wyoming, he bought another one in Lyman, Nebraska, where we grew sugar beets, field corn, alfalfa hay, and pinto beans. We drove tractors to cultivate the land, dug ditches in the fields for irrigation, actually did the irrigating, which back then was manual. Every day in the summer months, we walked up and down the fields with a shovel on our shoulder to irrigate and pump the tubes by hand to get the water in the ditches for the

4

fields. Our hands would be calloused and cracked from all the moisture and shoveling. We would have sold a sibling for the large, automated sprinklers that are used today.

When I was a freshman in high school, Dad bought a farm and planned to start a dairy about 40 minutes east of Minatare in Lyman, Nebraska. He was supplementing the family income by running a television repair shop, he also worked at the local television station as an engineer at night, and he had hopes the dairy farm would help support our large family, as well. My oldest sister and I worked on the farm in Minatare; our siblings worked on the farm in Lyman.

"Those cows aren't gonna milk themselves," Dad would holler at us around 3 a.m., as we scrambled out of our warm beds. When we came home from school in the afternoon, we milked the cows again and worked the sugar beet crops, leaving little time for extracurricular activities.

As anyone who has ever lived on a farm knows, farming is seven days a week. I often wondered how many people who bought food and milk understood what it took to get it to the grocery store. Farming is grueling work, and my siblings and I ended up developing a strong work ethic under Dad's tough tutelage.

In Lyman, my eight siblings and our parents were sardined into the two-bedroom, one bath house, so there was no room or reason to stay inside. Dad had us outside working, either with the cows or the crops, and he was a harsh boss. He didn't mince words or tolerate laziness or incompetence. Like a prison farm guard, Dad drilled his work ethic into us and used questionable means to get results. When I was eight years old and hoeing in the sugar beet field, he was dissatisfied with my labor. He marched over to me, pulled out a big wrench from his jeans pocket and walloped me on the leg, "You're cutting too many out, you stupid bitch!" he yelled.

He was angry a lot; I'm guessing it was from the financial strain of having such a large family. His anger was often directed at my siblings and me, and when he got going, it felt like a tornado was hitting our house. I didn't understand his stress or anger as an eight-year-old, and out in the field of sugar beets that day, I'm not sure which hurt most – the sting from being hit with a wrench or the sting of being called a stupid bitch.

Over the years of owning my company, we've employed hundreds of intelligent, enthusiastic people. I will always be grateful to Dad for instilling in me a strong work ethic, but I also learned from him to take really good care of my employees. Patience and kindness work a lot better than a wrench.

———■◦■———

Don't Tell Me I Can't

My dad and I had a thorny relationship. The constant conversation about what was not possible for the women in my family, and specifically me, ended up being a driving force for my success. Dad made his low opinion and expectations of me obvious, and I begrudgingly sought his approval by proving him wrong.

I used to dream that one day I would make millions and make my dad proud of me. I would tell him of all kinds of plans I had to become financially independent. Instead of engaging in the ideas and brainstorming the possibilities, he'd roll his eyes and respond, "Oh yeah? Ok kid." He predicted that I would marry an alcoholic and waitress my entire life.

When I was still in high school, I was sharing with him a new idea I had to make my millions. He had another idea: he would buy me a van so I could drive across the country, prostituting myself in order to raise money – of which he would take half.

My dad said such inappropriate things to me, it was heart-wrenching.

I don't know if these low expectations were bestowed on my siblings as well, but it was painful that my dad's opinion of my potential was so low. It was as if he was stamping my forehead with a big CAN'T to all of my ideas to make my millions.

I quit telling Dad of my career moves and dreams. I didn't want to hear it anymore. If his negative and inappropriate comments were his idea of a motivational talk, it was clear that career counseling was not in his wheelhouse.

There is no doubt that some of my bad choices and showing up hungover to work on the farm probably contributed to his opinion of me, but his limited view of my potential took up residence in my head that took years to overcome.

After a conversation with my grandma, Dad's mom, I began to understand that Dad had his own issues taking up space in his head, which most likely influenced his view of me.

My grandma and I were like two peas in a pod. We said she and I had the same genes. She was a superhero to me when I was young. Her home was immaculate. She had nice furniture that we couldn't sit on, and we couldn't wear our shoes in her house. She kept everything, including her car, clean and in perfect order, which was a striking contrast to our tiny house that burst at the seams with nine kids. I loved visiting her house. Besides the unconditional love she gave us, her home was a respite from the chaos and hard work that was a staple in our home.

Grandma was full of life; she was funny, healthy, happy, and loved to eat donuts and laugh. Often, I remember her saying, "As long as I can stand up and swing my arms up and down in the morning God has something he wants me to do today!"

She also loved to party and went out dancing and drinking nearly every night of her life. She said all her siblings, friends, and family told her she was going to drink herself to death. Adam, her husband of 60 years, would take care of her and her friends when they came home from the bar. Between getting sick, Grandma would make one of those empty alcoholic promises, "I'll never do this again."

Grandpa would respond, "You are a damn liar. You will do it again tonight."

My dad witnessed his mother's alcoholism and never drank as a result. One time my mom went drinking with my grandma and my dad told her if she ever did it again, he would leave her. I don't remember ever seeing either of them drink more than maybe a cocktail at a wedding. They probably couldn't afford to drink, but also, I think the actions of my grandma had a strong impact on my dad. I also think he saw the similarities in Grandma and me.

He never talked about it; nobody did. She finally told me, but not until I was older. She said after her 60th birthday party she got so sick that her doctor told her if she did not quit, she would die. She quit, never drinking alcohol again, and lived until a few days before her 100th birthday. Her cold-turkey quitting was an inspiration to me, and I thought of it often as I was fighting for a clean and sober life.

I held her hand when she passed away. With her last breath, she said, "One for the money, two for the show, three to get ready..." I completed her thought with, "Four to go, ready to go dancing. It is ok to go."

Fall 2002, I visited my parents, whose health was failing; my mom had been diagnosed with Alzheimer's a few years before and Dad had been dealing with colon cancer for the last couple of years. By then, I had made millions of dollars in revenue and given him two grandchildren, proving him wrong about my potential. As we talked, he took my hand and told me he was proud of me. For the first time in my life, he also told me that he loved me. He died in November 2002.

All of my siblings became successful at our separate pursuits, probably surpassing his expectations, but maybe not his dreams for us.

While it healed a portion of my heart to finally earn approval and love from Dad, by then I had learned to never let someone else define who I was or what I was capable of.

Life in Perspective

When we first moved to Torrington, Wyoming, I was my parents' sixth child and the youngest of five girls. Packed into our 1,000-square-foot house, the five girls shared one tiny bedroom. My brothers slept in the living room on a fold out sofa. When my baby sister arrived, she slept in a crib in our parents' room. In the girls' bedroom, two bunkbeds filled the room with a slender walking space between them. My four older sisters occupied the bunkbeds. I had a single, separate bed and felt very special that I didn't have to sleep in a bunkbed. I didn't have to climb up a ladder to get in bed; I didn't have another bed right on top of me; I had plenty of room to sit up. I had the best bed and I felt super special every night when I went to sleep.

Over time, my perspective of superiority due to my unique sleeping arrangements helped build my self-image; it became a touchstone for my confidence. As the youngest daughter of the first six and one of ultimately, nine kids, I had to compete for attention and individuality. My single bed reminded me each night that I was special. I even created a new name for myself when I was about five years old: Sandy Luck Luck, a reminder that I was a very lucky girl. Eventually, it helped give me the confidence to leave the farm and start a new life.

A few years ago, Martín, my current husband, and I were talking with my sisters, Annette and Tanya, and Martín mentioned that I had shared with him how my special bed helped bolster my self-confidence over the years. They laughed. Hard.

Catching her breath for a moment, Annette said, "Oh Sandra, your bed was *in the closet!*"

Closet???

I was stunned. All these years, my perspective on the sleeping arrangements was that I had the best bed; I was special. I'd completely blocked out that my bed had been relegated to the also-crowded closet. My perception of the "special" bed had bolstered my self-esteem and confidence *for years!*

Sometimes our perspectives serve us better than reality.

Introduction to Insecurity

When I was about 10 years old, I smoked my first cigarette and drank alcohol, like a middle-aged divorcée trying to forget her circumstances. We had moved from Torrington, Wyoming to Minatare, Nebraska, not by choice but because the farm went bankrupt. I remember a man coming to the door and telling Dad we had to be off the property by the following week.

"Where am I going to go with all these kids?" pleaded my dad. "I need more time."

The banker said he was sorry, but just repeated that we had to be out in a week.

There was a big rush to pack everything while Dad and Mom went searching for a place for us to land on short notice. They found a big two-story house about 45 minutes away in Minatare. This is where Dad took a job as an electrical engineer at the local television station, opened a TV repair shop and started renting farmland to rebuild and start over.

We were quickly enrolled in new schools, leaving our familiar surroundings and friends behind. My earlier feeling of being special and confident took a detour when we moved. A big helping of insecurity also ushered in an addiction that would dictate my life for the coming years.

At my school, I didn't fit in with the popular kids and my only friend was Tammy, who lived across the street from us. She was being raised by a single mother who worked all day, so Tammy came home to an empty house. She started inviting me over and eventually, we got into her mother's vodka and cigarettes. I learned that after drinking vodka, I no longer cared about the new school, the popular kids, or where I was. While I didn't really like the taste or burning sensation of the cigarettes, we thought we looked cool smoking them.

We would trade clothes, smoke and drink for our lunch break. After one of our "lunch breaks" when we returned to school, her house caught on fire. We could see it from our classroom, and we were afraid one of us had forgotten to put out a cigarette. Plus, I was wearing Tammy's clothes and mine were now fuel for the fire. I knew I was going to be in trouble one way or another when I got home. It turned out it was an electrical fire; not caused by a forgotten cigarette. But I still got in trouble for wearing Tammy's clothes and being at her house, instead of school.

I continued smoking off and on until I was 23 years old, when I quit cold turkey. But I spent the next 15 years escalating my drinking, then added drugs to my method of coping.

When I went through puberty and developed a figure, all of the sudden I became attractive to the popular kids. I was invited to parties at their houses, where I learned how to smoke weed.

In high school, my older, male cousin took me to parties where I was introduced to a variety of drugs including yellow jackets, white cross and black beauties – all variations of speed. Cocaine was just a short step away, and I took it.

Both alcohol, weed and drugs were readily available, and I found dating drug dealers made it even easier – and cheaper – to keep me in the popular group and keep my insecurities at bay.

On the Move

The day I graduated from high school my dad asked me if I would be drinking Jose Cuervo and dancing on the tables. I responded with a flippant, "Maybe." Throughout high school, I partied pretty hard, and I was dating a drug dealer, so his question wasn't out of nowhere. I was his mom's granddaughter, after all.

My partying continued after graduation, staying out all night and getting home at 3:30 a.m. to milk cows. I would fall asleep standing up, leaning on a table or post. Finally, dad said that arrangement wasn't working for him anymore.

"When I find you leaning on things and falling asleep, I want to move them out from under you so you fall down and hit your head," he said. "So kid, you gotta go." That was his way of telling me I needed to move out.

As if Dad's prediction of my pathetic future was about to come true, I packed up my clothes and Smokey, my cat, and moved in with my drug dealer boyfriend, who lived in a trailer park. But dad underestimated my drive for something better.

Somehow, I was able to get employment as a teller at a bank, which was a big step up from milking cows, in my opinion, and it paid my expenses. Unfortunately, my boyfriend could not keep a job. It became an issue for me, since I came from a family where everyone pulled their weight. I guess hearing me bug him about it must have been an even bigger issue for him, because one day I came home from work to find all my things outside on the front deck. Smokey was tied to the deck with a piece of twine. Not knowing what to do I reluctantly called my dad. He came and got my stuff with a gun on his pickup truck seat in case there was a confrontation with my now ex-boyfriend.

I moved in with two women, one was a hairdresser, and one was a nurse; both worked long, hard hours. I had to get a second job to cover my expenses with my unexpected and upgraded move, so I took a job at Godfathers Pizza, working every night. I knew that I would always be able to eat as I could have a mini pizza, all the salad bar and soda that I wanted for each shift.

The bank required me to take a two-week vacation each year, so when I had worked long enough to earn those two weeks, I wasn't sure what to do with the time. My friend, Kerry, who was confined to a wheelchair due to a bad car accident, asked me to go with him to Arizona and California. I'd never been out of Nebraska, so I was mentally packing my bag before he finished inviting me.

We stayed with his cousin in Manhattan Beach where I wheeled him down to the beach and we both got our first look at the Pacific Ocean. In Phoenix, we stayed in a really cheap motel because it had a swimming pool. Basking in the sun by the pool, we felt like we were living a good life. Before our vacation ended, I already had a plan to move to Phoenix.

I knew that working two jobs, living paycheck to paycheck, I would never be able to save enough for a move out of state, so my friend, Kerry, ended up loaning me $10,000 to buy 11 dairy cattle that were pregnant. I became acutely aware of my sales talent when I got my dad to agree that I could move back to the farm with the cattle and exchange rent for labor.

My cows gave birth to healthy baby calves. Plus, after giving birth is when a cow produces the most milk, so that provided a little more income. But shortly after, my dad said, "Hey kid, I thought you wanted to move to Arizona." I said I did.

"Well, it is time for you to go," he said.

After a week or two after that conversation he said, "Hey kid, I thought you were going to Phoenix." Knowing it was his way of telling me to move, I asked, "When?"

"Now," he said. What my dad wasn't telling me is that he was about to file bankruptcy and lose the farm again…which is why he wanted me to go. I thought he just wanted me to take my partying-self somewhere else.

I sold my calves, profiting just over $900. I then stuffed all my belongings and cat into my 1978 Toyota Celica and a small U-Haul and left Lyman, NE. I drove to Lincoln to party with a couple of friends that were attending the University of Nebraska. I then drove to Denver, stopping to party with more friends. By the time I left for Arizona, I only had a gun with a sawed-off penny for the scope on top of the pistol (given to me by one of my friends) and $400 in my pocket.

By the way, I still owed Kerry for the loan to buy the cows. I'd only made a couple of payments to him. His mom asked how and when I was going to pay him back and I said, "I don't know. I'm going to Phoenix and get a job."

I drove through a blizzard at night leaving Denver, following semi-trucks during the blizzard that night to get up the hills and over the mountains. It was white-knuckle driving like I'd never experienced,

17

and when I finally got to Albuquerque, New Mexico, I pulled off the side of the road and slept a little. I was exhausted.

When I woke up my car would not start. Bolstered by the knowledge that I had a gun in the car (even though I didn't know how to use it), I walked over to a truck and asked the driver to help me start the car. He turned out to be very kind and helpful and I followed him to Flagstaff. He continued his route, but I stopped at a Super 8 motel. He even called me to make sure I was ok.

The next morning, I drove into Phoenix and a new chapter of my life began.

———◆◆———

Reality Sets In

As I arrived in Phoenix, I pulled off the freeway on Thomas Road and saw an apartment for rent sign. I stopped and within the hour I was unloading the U-Haul into my newly rented apartment. Suddenly, the move was a reality. A new state; a new city; no job; and not much money. I was exhausted and scared. I walked to a pay phone, called my parents and started crying.

"Kid," my dad said. "If you bit off more than you can chew, you can always come back."

His words and tone of his voice were a challenge to me. Knowing he didn't want me back any more than I wanted to go back, I stopped crying.

"I'm not coming back," I stiffly replied. "I'm just tired, but I'm fine." I hung up the phone, walked back to my apartment, and smoked a joint with a neighbor I just met.

I found a job almost as quickly as I found my apartment. A co-worker from the bank in Nebraska had moved to Phoenix, so I called her the next day and we agreed to meet for lunch. As I was leaving her office, I stopped to look at the pond with beautiful koi fish outside the building.

"Hey doll," a voice said. "What are you doing?" I turned to see a man standing a few feet away. Nobody had ever called me 'doll' before; I was flattered but stayed on task.

"Looking for a job," I responded. He told me his office was looking for a receptionist.

"Come tomorrow and meet with our accounting manager for an interview," he suggested. He wrote down the name and suite number of the building.

I got the job, which paid $450 a month. It seemed like the pay was low, but I needed money right away. I later learned the former receptionist, who had been promoted, had been earning $950 a month for that same job. When I asked my boss for more money, he told me I was on probation for 90 days; after that we would revisit the issue.

On the 90th day I followed up with him.

"What do you need more money for?" he asked. "You only have rent to pay right?"

"I suppose if I don't eat, shower, turn on lights, make car payments, or use my car, yeah, I only have rent to pay, asshole," I said to myself.

Job hunting became my new priority.

———◈———

Living the High Life

While I found a job right away, it also didn't take me long to find some drugs. I was introduced to Mike by someone in a club. He was not only a dealer, but he was a pilot who moved drugs, as well. We started dating and I enjoyed the high life that comes with dating someone who made a lot of money dealing drugs.

We flew to Las Vegas to party; he bought me a sports car; moved me into a cool apartment filled with furniture I picked out, but he paid for it. The drug-fueled life was a whirlwind, and I had no idea what was going to happen next. It was exciting. Until he disappeared.

Since the time I met Mike, we were constantly in touch. If we weren't together physically, we would be on the phone making plans to be together. When I didn't hear from him for a couple of days, I thought it was odd, but didn't worry about it. When it became a week, I started worrying that he'd been in a plane crash or arrested. I went to the clubs, thinking I would find him there, but instead, I learned that Mike went back to his ex-wife and his two young kids.

Surprises like that provided me with just the excuse I needed to binge on more drugs. Conveniently, one of the benefits of dating a drug dealer is that you meet other drug dealers, so I had plenty of connections where I could get more drugs; I didn't need Mike, I told myself.

With the consumption of more drugs and alcohol to forget how I'd been ghosted, I didn't go to work consistently, and I was rarely on time, if I did show up. It didn't take long before I lost my job. I stopped paying my bills, got evicted from my cool apartment, and I got really paranoid.

Friends of Mike's, a dentist and his wife, let me move into a house they owned in a part of Phoenix that was not great, but it was rent-free. They also gave me a job as a dental assistant. The first day on the job I showed up hungover. The dentist needed my help with a patient. She was getting dentures, so he had to extract all of her teeth. The fact that she was a drug addict made it a tricky procedure.

In my hungover state, I got the shakes, and it was so bad, the dentist had to call the lab tech to help him instead. The dentist and I fought sometimes because he thought I wasn't doing my best at the job he had given me. I had a hard time arguing that fact, because working hard and doing your best was drilled into my head on the farm. I knew I wasn't doing a good job, but I had become a slave to my drug habit, and I wasn't able or willing to be responsible for my situation. To make myself not feel bad, I just did more drugs.

Predictably, my multiple second chances wore out with the dentist and his wife, and I lost my job and rent-free home. With no home, I walked around Phoenix at night paranoid, high or feeling sorry for myself. I wondered if I would learn from this and do something different in the future.

My friend, Linda, came to my rescue. She and her husband were having financial problems, and she was getting a divorce. I moved into an apartment with her and her two young kids. She got a job as a dancer at a strip club, and I got another job so I could pay rent and my bills.

Linda and I began partying together, which made it difficult for me to show up to my job again. I met Jimmy through my manicurist, Cynthia. She was dating Brian, his best friend and landscape business partner. They were in great shape and tan from working outside and shimmying up palm trees. Turns out they were drug addicts and some of their jobs were paid out in drugs instead of cash, but most jobs were paid in cash so they could always get drugs.

It didn't take long before I had a new job helping them with manual labor picking up the palm fronds and putting them in the back of the truck to take to the dump. It was a cash business, and we were paid daily so we could get high. I always thought I was not as bad as them because they were shooting drugs; I was not using in that way. Yet.

Predictably, my drug-using boyfriend and my excessive partying became more than Linda bargained for and she locked me out of the apartment. When I arrived home, she wasn't there, so I had Joey, another drug dealer friend who was a big guy, kick the door in. It didn't occur to me that might have freaked Linda and her kids out to come home to a kicked-in front door. The police were called, but because I lived there, they didn't do anything.

Soon after that incident, Jimmy and I got an apartment together and in a rare sober moment, we discussed getting real jobs with insurance and starting a family. I had always had an entrepreneurial spirit, and we made a plan to sell drugs to make money. Today, it sounds crazy just to write that down.

The only problem we could see was whether we made money or borrowed money from a financial institution or a friend. Surprisingly to us, we couldn't get a loan from a bank, since we had no real jobs, income, or credit. We bought what we could with the money we scraped together, and we had lofty intentions about the amount of money we were going to make.

Instead, we used the drugs to celebrate our new business venture.

After coming down from our three-day bender of being high, with no money and no food, I was so hungry, I went to the dumpster to get a bag of stale tortilla chips from the garbage. I put them on the barbeque grill in hopes of making them taste less stale. My culinary experiment did not work, the chips were still stale, and I ended up throwing them back in the dumpster. What were we thinking about starting a drug business and family?

While I was using drugs, my ability to reason, communicate, and function as a human being were greatly compromised. At one point, Joey owed me a debt and wouldn't pay it up. Angry and high, I showed up at his house with a little stick of dynamite that Mike had given me when we were dating. I set it off in Joey's front yard. The sound of the dynamite blast brought Joey out of his house to settle his debt, but it also brought the police. They said someone reported a gun shot.

Unfortunately, the gun my friend from Nebraska had given me before I left town was sitting on the front seat of my car and for a moment, I feared I may be headed to jail. The police checked it and could tell that it had not been fired. I told them I had just moved to Phoenix from Nebraska and that my friend had given me the gun for protection during the move. I confessed I also didn't know how to use the gun. They shook their heads and left after telling me to be careful.

Sandy Luck Luck still had it.

———◼ ❙ ◼———

A Career is Born

I was an addict, but I was in deep denial. Rather than admit my own addiction, I focused on Jimmy's excessive drug use because admittedly, his addiction had led to other drugs and more erratic behavior than mine. But as long as I focused on his problems, I could avoid looking at what I was doing. In a moment of semi-clarity, I decided it would be best for me to break up with Jimmy, so he could quit ruining my life.

I moved to Fort Collins, Colorado, where my high school friend, Tari, lived with her husband. She probably saved my life by helping me start over. They let me stay with them for free, lent me money, and helped me get a car by verifying my employment at her nail salon.

Amazingly, I then got a job with Factual Data, my first taste of the information business. Tired of being poor and hungry, I decided I was going to establish credit and build a good life. I threw myself into my job and even took a second job working at The Wine Cellar, a fine dining restaurant and bar; I was the hostess at night. One night I was asked to help with waitressing in the bar because they were short-handed. I agreed, even though I was petrified. I had never opened a bottle of wine and the restaurant was named The Wine Cellar for a reason,

I prayed no one would order a bottle of wine in my section. One of my first tables ordered a shrimp appetizer and I put the order in at the kitchen window and went to take another order. When I returned,

I saw a plate with shrimp on it, so I delivered it to my table. A few minutes later, one of the other servers came into the bar and saw my table enjoying the shrimp scampi that his table of six had ordered.

"You gave those people MY shrimp scampi!" he screamed at me. "You will never make it as a server here."

I went in the bathroom and cried. That was the end of my waitress career. I guess my dad was wrong, I would not be working as a waitress my whole life.

Although I did not give up the alcohol and drugs yet, I had taken an interest in the information business and was showing up for work consistently and mostly on time.

Then Jimmy showed up in Fort Collins. I guess I had not had enough of his drama, so I let him back into my life. He got a job and for a few months we were both working and getting along great. It didn't take long, however, that he got antsy and decided to take a trip back to Phoenix to see his family. He said he would be gone two weeks. He never came back.

When I first realized he wasn't returning, it brought back the feeling of being deserted by Mike. I felt traumatized. In the short time Jimmy had been in Fort Collins, it seemed like we might be able to build a life together, but neither of us had made any attempt at getting clean and sober. We were still the same messed up people, so it was no surprise, really, that it imploded.

Jimmy was gone long enough for me to realize that I could make it on my own. He did try to come back months later, but I was done. I felt like I was on a new path, and I didn't want anything to distract me.

Opportunities are always knocking when we least expect it. I wanted to get into sales and Factual Data was trying to expand, so the company was opening offices to franchise in different locations. I asked if I could start one for them as a salesperson. I had been promoted to manager and my work ethic had finally kicked in. My drug use was limited to off hours and weekends. They agreed, but I would have to move...to Phoenix.

While I wasn't eager to return to Phoenix, I didn't want to pass up the opportunity. So, I went for it. The only friends I had there were Lisa and those I had partied with.

Before I started in sales, Marsha, one of the owners of Factual Data, sat me down and told me that I should look at what other successful salespeople looked like and wear what they wear if I wanted to be successful in sales. I took note, then took inventory of my closet. I had two suits at the time, one was turquoise (which I thought would be great in Phoenix!) and the other was a tan linen suit. I loved both of them. My linen suit passed Marsha's fashion judgment, but when she saw the turquoise suit, she said, "Maybe not something so bright."

Crushed, I turned to my mom, explaining my disappointment that I couldn't wear my turquoise suit anymore.

"You have always been a bright and cheerful girl, Sandra," she said. "It is ok you have bright things." A mother's love, right?

Turned out, I was good in sales. I enjoyed cold calling and getting new customers for the mortgage credit reporting. At that time, I took the reports to my executive suite and faxed them to Factual Data's Colorado office. They would do the reports, send them back to me, and I would hand deliver them all over Phoenix and Scottsdale. I started to build the business.

I was the poster child for a functioning addict.

———◄◗►———

Panic Attack & 30-Day Chips

I wanted to treat my move back to Phoenix as another new start, party-wise. I really wanted to be clean and sober, and I knew it would be essential to my work success. My past efforts at becoming clean and sober had been futile. I could rarely string together more than 30 days with no drugs or alcohol. If somehow, I did white-knuckle a month together, my friends and I went out and partied to celebrate the milestone.

The next morning, I'd be back on Day One. I accumulated multiple 30-day chips, stringing so many of them together I could have made a garland.

Sadly, I knew if I was serious about getting clean and sober, I would have to avoid my party friends who were still using. I knew it would be difficult to maintain sobriety if I was around the drugs and alcohol. I decided to try to make some new friends.

I met Rhonda, who worked for a bank on Camelback Road that did mortgage loans. She was my client and we started getting together for happy hour after work. We were young and both trying to get ahead at our jobs. We had fun together. We each had a friend named Lisa that we talked about but neither of us knew the other one was doing drugs with their friend Lisa.

Eventually, we decided to get an apartment together in Scottsdale. I was excited because I thought Rhonda would be a good influence on me. As it turns out, the first night that we met at our new place, we were both high. Like me, she sometimes became paranoid when she got high, but her paranoia was followed by a serious panic attack, which kicked in at the new apartment.

I didn't know what to do. She was shaking; her heart was racing, and she was getting dizzy and sweating. She finally called her mom, which almost set me into a panic mode. What would her mom do when she got to the apartment and found both of us high?

Her mom arrived, calmed Rhonda down, and told us that the next day we were going to a meeting. I didn't know what meeting she had in mind, and she didn't elaborate. All I knew was, according to Rhonda's mom, *we would be at that meeting.*

It turned out to be the first CA (Cocaine Anonymous) meeting either of us had ever attended. It was held in a non-descript room of a church conference center. The seats were filled with addicts who shared their various stages of recovery with the group. I wondered if anyone could tell that I had used before coming to the meeting.

Glancing around the room, I was fascinated with the variety of people who were there. Men and women, some who looked wealthy; some who looked like they couldn't even afford the one-dollar donation. There were members of the group who were perfectly coiffed and dressed in designer clothes, sitting next to some who looked like they slept under a bridge the night before. I was taking everyone's inventory while the leader of the group was explaining the rules. That's probably why I didn't hear him say you shouldn't share if you had used in the last 24 hours. Unfortunately, I heard him say just the opposite, so I shared, pouring out my heart as only someone who is high can do. Rhonda and her mom were horrified, while others looked at me knowingly.

Rhonda's mom said we had to keep going back if we were going to keep the apartment. I was kind of hoping after my "share" the group wouldn't let us back in, but that wasn't the case. In fact, everyone was very welcoming to us, which scared me. I started feeling accountable about drugs for the first time in my life.

Again and again, I would get 30 days sober and then go to happy hour to celebrate. Every time I drank, I would turn to drugs, as well. They went together like peanut butter and jelly. After one meeting on a Friday night when I got one of my 30-day chip, I announced I was going to celebrate and go to happy hour. A woman came up to me afterward.

"You do not get it," she said. "This is abstinence from *all* mind-altering substances. That includes alcohol."

That hadn't occurred to me. But, I replied, "Alcohol isn't a problem for me."

"One leads to the other," she said.

I didn't believe her because I was still a know-it-all expert. So, I went to happy hour, only to disappoint myself again by chasing alcohol with drugs.

Rhonda and I supported each other. We both tried to stay clean and sober and kept going back to meetings. One night, Rhonda became fearful, and she came into my bedroom on the verge of another panic attack. I had been asleep, but she woke me up.

"Sandra, I'm scared. Do you have any cocaine?" she asked in a shaky voice.

"I don't. What's going on?" I responded.

"I just need something to stop my mind from racing and I'm scared," she said.

"Come and lie down," I said, flipping back the covers on my bed. She crawled into bed with me, and we talked until we both fell asleep.

That happened a number of times for both of us. If one of us would get scared or paranoid, we could get in bed with the other one so we could help calm each other down. It worked well and helped keep us clean.

If Rhonda's mom hadn't come to save her daughter from a panic attack that night in our new apartment, I may not be sober today. She inadvertently saved me, too. That experience was a gift to my life that I did not understand at the time.

It was not easy; I get why they say take it one day at a time.

———◆———

Double Responsibilities

Shortly after realizing I wasn't really working Cocaine Anonymous like I needed, I got serious and found a sponsor. I started working the steps and attending meetings every day, sometimes more than one a day. To supplement my salary at Factual Data, I worked evenings at Abco Deli and Bakery at night. Keeping busy helped keep me sober and kept me from spending money, so I was able to pay off debts that I acquired while using. Each night, I closed the bakery and hosed it down with a big power washer hose, like the one we used in the dairy barn in Nebraska. Funny how we can move far away and still end up doing the same thing. I think in the 12-Step program, they call that "pulling a geographic."

The owner of Factual Data and I ended up having a disagreement because I thought with more responsibility, I should get paid more. He disagreed and called me a bitch. At least he didn't hit me with a wrench when he said it. But I wasn't eight years old; I could leave. And so, I did.

I took my turquoise suit to Mortgage Information Services, which hired me right away. I was eager to prove myself and I threw all my energy into selling the services. We started growing quickly, to the point that the operation couldn't support the sales I was bringing in. I was asked to manage the operation and do sales for less money.

I felt like I was experiencing déjà vu. Why didn't anyone want to pay for the added responsibility? I reluctantly agreed, just to get the operations experience, but I was not happy I was doing two jobs for the price of one.

While meeting with a client of mine, I shared that I was now also in charge of operations.

"Are you being compensated for the added work?" my client asked. I shared with him my dissatisfaction with the non-reward.

"Why don't you just start your own company?" he asked.

"That takes either money or credit, which I don't have," I replied.

"That will show up," he said.

I was cautiously hopeful. And I promised myself that if I was fortunate enough to start my own business, I wouldn't ask employees to double-up on responsibilities without providing a growth path or incentive or both for them to do the work.

———◗❙◖———

Clean and Sober

Working in information services had opened my eyes to possibilities I could never see before. It was interesting to me how the credit industry worked. I learned how important good credit is and the effect it can have on my life. The second job had provided a way for me to pay off debts, and once that was done, I opened a bank account and started saving whatever I could.

Eventually, I was able to start building credit. The first credit card I got was to buy a new king-size bed at a department store. Back then, upgrading my bed from the half of the bunk bed that came with me from the farm was a priority. It symbolized "my arrival." As the money accumulated in my bank account, I developed a new goal: wealth. I was obsessed with seeing what I could do next.

Starting my own business turned out to be the next step. I saw how the other companies were operating, and I had an idea of how I could do it better. I just didn't think I had enough money saved yet to strike out on my own. To my surprise, one of the owners of Mortgage Information Services, and his wife, lent me $10,000 to start my own company.

Residential Mortgage Credit Reporting (RMCR) launched on September 2, 1989, in Phoenix. He and I agreed if he was not competing with me in a year, we would be partners. After a year, he was still competing with me so we agreed I could buy him out instead.

He and his wife are on my forever gratitude list; they believed in me when I did not yet have the confidence.

By this time, I had more than a year of sobriety. Work replaced drugs and alcohol and I grew the business fast, without any other outside funding. I used cash flow to build the business and focused on getting paid fast. Soon, I was billing over a million dollars in revenue and was growing the team to more than 50 people. I moved from the little red house I started in on Central Avenue in Phoenix to 100 W. Clarendon Avenue, a high-rise building. From my office window, I could see an S on a nearby hill, which I felt was prophetic.

While I enjoyed seeing my initials on the hill, the landmark also brought back memories of Mike. That's where I stayed after being ghosted by him. Mike did reappear eventually, feeling guilty. Not because he disappeared on me, but because he felt like he was responsible for me becoming an addict. To be honest, I was an addict before I ever met him. At one time, Mike gave me money so I could go to real estate school to become a realtor, but I only used the money on drugs.

Unfortunately, Mike died in a tragic accident. He was loading his helicopter on a trailer to be taken to Florida and he hit some power lines. He died shortly after being taken to the hospital. Because at that point, I was clean and sober, I was able to attend his funeral. It was still emotional, but I didn't need drugs to cope with it…and I was grateful. As it turns out, I was also grateful that he reunited with his family so they could have those last few years with him before he passed.

After about a year and a half, I only went to meetings on occasion to celebrate an anniversary or to support someone else that asked to me go with them. I was so busy working on the business and myself, the desire to use drugs and alcohol had left me.

There were new challenges in my life and running RMCR was so fulfilling to me, I no longer felt the need for drugs and alcohol to build my confidence or make my life interesting. I was no longer dating drug dealers; I was away from people who were telling me I wasn't enough or couldn't do something; I was successfully running a company; and I had an income that was finally fulfilling my dreams.

Today, I have 36 years of sobriety from both alcohol and drugs and the desire to use has not returned regardless of the challenges I have had.

I'm grateful for it every day.

———◖ ◗———

Becoming Accountable

In the 12-step program, it is considered unwise to start dating anyone in the first year of sobriety. They reason the emotional ups and downs, and fragile state of sobriety isn't conducive to building a new relationship. Nothing is said about starting a new business.

So, shortly after starting RMCR, someone who was watching me closely suggested strongly that I contact Becky Robbins, a highly recommended life coach. I was eager to get all the help I could, so I hired her not knowing what to expect. After talking several times, she suggested that I do some personal and professional growth training with Landmark Worldwide, a company that offers development programs to help individuals be more effective in the important areas of their life.

Working with Landmark changed my life. I learned about being accountable for myself and everything that happens to me, regardless of who, what, where or when. I found out that there is power in being accountable; that by choosing to be accountable mountains could be moved in a short period of time.

In learning to be accountable, something had been eating at me is that I still owed Kerry money for the cows I bought in Nebraska. I called him and asked him what I needed to pay him so we would be good. He gave me the number and I sent a check that day to him overnight.

We've been good ever since. In taking accountability for everything in my life, this was a good step.

One of the struggles that I experienced when I first started hiring people was my high expectation for them to care as much as I did about the success of RMCR. I also expected employees to be as dependable as I was. It was frustrating to me when employees made mistakes or didn't show up. I would lose my temper often. Becky helped me to learn that no matter what challenge occurs, it can be fixed -- God can fix it, someone can fix it, and someone has probably fixed it before me. This helped me to grow my optimism and continue to grow the company. She has worked with me over the years off and on. She has always been available to me, and I will always be grateful for her love and support.

Like peeling an onion, I found there are multiple layers of learning humility and asking for help when I need it. Fortunately, I am always blessed with meeting wonderful, intelligent people who are willing to share their knowledge when I do seek that help.

Giving Back

In addition to the Landmark program, Becky Robbins told me I needed to get involved with my community and give back. She introduced me to Phoenix Youth at Risk and said serving there would not only be good for the teen I was partnered with, but it would also help my community and me. Mitch Akin ran the program and he was blind. It took me years to completely understand why Mitch matched me with a teenage boy that came from a troubled home, but when I met 13-year-old Aaron Spaulding, we both looked each other in the eyes and held hands and cried.

My agreement was to be an adult that Aaron could count on. All the kids did a weeklong program and at the end of the week, they met a committed partner, an adult who provided them with support for the next six months. He could call me to talk to me, but I agreed not to give him money or buy him things; only be there if he needed support. I would pick him up every Wednesday night and take him to a Youth at Risk meeting. They talked about challenges and did exercises in communicating at the meetings. He and I would talk afterward.

Aaron would also call me when he needed to talk or ask my advice on a decision he needed to make. Sometimes, he would just call to process something. Many times, we ate meals together as we talked.

When Aaron joined the Navy, he was deployed with the Marines as a med tech in Iraq and Afghanistan four different times. He helped to save a lot of lives. He finally retired from the Navy after 22 years. Officially, I only committed to working with Aaron for six months, but he still considers me his committed partner today, 35 years later.

When I was going through my divorce, Aaron told me that he thought my ex-husband made me forget who I was. He told me I was still great, which helped bolster my confidence at the time. I know I can count on him, and he knows he can count on me, if he or his family needs anything. It is a love that was built on trust and consistency.

Getting involved in charitable work was a huge blessing to me and I continue to find organizations, projects, or other ways I can be of service. We do not have to look far to find someone who has more challenges than we do, and when we help others, it takes our focus away from our own challenges and makes them smaller.

Helping v. Selling

One day, a large banking client called me and said her friend, Jill, needed my help and asked me to please call her. She didn't give me any details about why Jill needed my help, and I didn't ask. Since getting clean and sober, I received calls for help from other members of CA, AA and NA. Was Jill an addict and needed to be escorted to a meeting?

I called her right away and we made plans to meet in person the following day. I was ready with a list of meetings for her, my own story, and encouragement to get clean and sober.

Fortunately, an intervention was not what Jill needed. Her company provided employees to IBM, and they needed to be background checked. She said it was taking over a month to get these done through a huge organization she was using, and she was losing candidates. Relieved this wasn't a call for help with an addiction, I changed gears, and we talked about what searches she needed.

I returned to my office and talked with my team. The next day I called her and outlined a plan showing her how RMCR could help her. She became our first client for employee background checks, a service that was an open field and very profitable in 1996. Realizing the opportunity with this new service stream, I soon got a second client by making cold calls. I felt like I had struck a gold vein in the information service business, as we added more background check clients very quickly.

My good friend, Arlene, who has been in business more than 50 years, always says the more you give the more you get. I have always admired her outlook on business, and she has been a wonderful mentor to me.

What sticks with me about this experience to this day, is that I didn't meet Jill to try to sell her anything; I was meeting to *help* her. Like Arlene has taught me, it was through my willingness to be helpful to someone else that I received so much in return -- which continues to this day. *Helping* our clients, instead of *selling* them, has become my calling card ever since.

High Expectations

In the HBO documentary Becoming Warren Buffett, the legendary investor gave some marital advice that I wish I had heard before I walked down the aisle for the first time. For a lasting marriage, he recommended marrying someone with low expectations. When I first heard that, it made me laugh. Who is looking for a partner with low expectations? What does that even look like? However, contemplating my two marriages and how different they are, I no longer laugh at that comment; I nod my head in solidarity that only comes from experience.

At the time I met Steve, my first husband, I was running Residential Mortgage Credit Reporting (RMCR) in Phoenix. It was a heady time for me – I was clean and sober, had a growing bank account, a house, and my business had more than $1.5 million in revenue. I could barely believe how much my life had changed as I was leaving my 20s. But it was about to change even more.

A friend and I were networking at a conference in Phoenix when Steve walked into the room. In the past, my friend had dated him, and I could understand why – he was super handsome, confident, and intelligent.

Steve asked my friend to introduce us, and we talked about our businesses. He asked if he could visit my office to see how it operated. He and his friend were interested in opening the same business in California, so we made plans for him to come back to Phoenix. He stayed for a week, and we met every day at my office. I enjoyed showing off the business that I built, and like I said, he was easy on the eyes, so I didn't mind his presence in the office. He then went back to the Bay Area and started the same business with his friend/partner.

At the end of the week, he said he'd like to take me to dinner…as a date. I turned him down because I wasn't interested in a casual date. I was starting to feel like it was time to find someone to build a life with and I didn't even consider that with Steve….at first.

He continued to call me, and we would get together whenever he visited Phoenix. When he wasn't in Phoenix we talked on the telephone several times a week. Steve was a master-pursuer. He asked me out all the time. I was a challenge for him and the more I said no, the more he pursued me.

Eventually, we agreed to date and see each other every other week at least, we agreed we would take turns flying back and forth between the San Francisco Bay Area and Phoenix. He never really liked the heat in Phoenix but we both agreed to the arrangement to see how it would go.

Steve was a big step up from the kind of men I had dated my whole life, and I became fascinated with him, like a kid staring at an exotic animal at the zoo. Steve didn't sell or do drugs! He rarely drank alcohol! He had good credit! (I checked). Like a former boyfriend, he was a pilot, but instead of running drugs, Steve flew helicopters for the Airforce National Guard and saved people's lives; he was a rescue helicopter pilot. He was college educated. He and his business partner were operating a successful company. He was reliable, had integrity and wasn't gay or married. To top it off, we were both from the Midwest. These were all good signs for me, and after a couple of years of dating we agreed over one of our telephone conversations to become engaged.

Here's the background to that conversation. My younger brother called me to let me know he was getting married and asked me to be in the wedding party. I was super happy for him and excited to be in his wedding. But when we hung up, it hit me that I was the only sibling in my family, other than the baby, that wasn't married. I started crying and wondered," What's wrong with me???"

I called Steve and, in my tears, told him I was not going to fly to California for a date anymore. "Why not?" he asked. "What do you want? Do you want to get engaged?"

I said, "Yes. Why would I fly to California for a *date*? I can get a date here in Phoenix."

"OK, we're engaged," he replied.

Later, Steve used to tell everyone that he got engaged under duress on the phone. According to Oxford Languages, the definition of duress is threats, violence, constraints, or other action brought to bear on someone to do something against their will or better judgment.

Pissed me off. Yellow flag.

If I had looked up the definition back then, I probably wouldn't have walked down that aisle.

We never really talked about hard issues that married couples typically face. Both of us were excellent negotiators, so surely, we could figure things out as they came up, right? Since Steve surpassed my low bar of good credit and not selling or using drugs, I wasn't concerned with much else.

Before we even signed the marriage paperwork, we bought a beautiful house in California and began living together. I became a regular on the Southwest flight to and from Phoenix as I commuted from California to work. I should have noticed I was the one commuting, not Steve.

Our military wedding, which I paid for, was breathtaking, with Steve and his friends in uniform, the groomsmen in white gloves and a saber arch when we left the church. The wedding took place at Xavier Catholic Church in Phoenix, followed by a reception at a Commemorative Air Force Museum in Chandler, Arizona. We had bubble gum pink roses on the tables with the beautiful table clothes. The hangar doors were open and at sunset we started to celebrate with a plane coming in for a landing at sunset. My mom, dad, grandma, sister, Tanya, her family, and my younger brothers attended. The day was perfect.

I was practically giddy in my high expectations, believing I had just married the perfect match for building a great future and an empire together.

But we got off to a rocky start. The limo did not come back to pick up the bride and groom after the reception. I ended up driving my new husband and the best man back to the Ritz Carlton Hotel, where we were staying.

As I was packing for our honeymoon, I realized I had left my passport at my office. We were leaving the next morning for Cancun, so I had to get it that night. Steve was mad that I had forgotten it and begrudgingly went with me to go retrieve it in the middle of the night.

When we got to Cancun, we spent the first three days looking for a cheaper place to stay. Steve had booked the Ritz Carlton in Cancun but was concerned about money. Annoyed, I finally said, "I'm not doing this on our honeymoon. You have your whole life to pay off the honeymoon. Let's enjoy the time while we're here."

The most amazing memory of the honeymoon was going scuba diving, I cannot swim so after going down 18 feet successfully, I was ramped up and felt like it was the best life ever.

From that point on, we had a good time, which led me to believe, like any new bride, that we found our happy ending.

I was so naïve.

The Lost Empire

As I was navigating a new marriage, my company was doing well. It was running smoothly, and we steadily took on more clients and created new, innovative services. I was happy to have a life partner to share confidential business information with freely and I often shared ideas and details with my husband.

Steve had sold his company and was taking a year off. It was 1996 and we had already been married for two years. He was now figuring out what he wanted to do next. Life was good.

RMCR had just won a couple of new accounts based on our innovative way of doing quick background checks and I was proud of my team for developing my idea and anticipated the possibilities it was already bringing. I could hardly wait to tell Steve about it. This could be the family business empire that I wanted to build with Steve.

We were heading out the next day on vacation in Florida, so I waited to tell him until we got there, so we could celebrate. He listened with interest and congratulated me on coming up with the idea. During our vacation, Steve called his former business partner, and I overheard him saying they should start a company that does background checks. He then outlined my idea of how to go about it. I was stunned. While we hadn't talked yet about this becoming a family business, and we never verbally said details about each other's businesses shouldn't be discussed outside our marriage, I expected that to be the case.

When he finished his call, I confronted him about sharing the confidential information and suggested we build this new business together. He declined and said there was enough business for both of us. I was hurt he didn't want to work with me to build a family business – our empire – together. I was also annoyed that Steve took my idea and was planning to start a competing company with someone else.

<hr>

Yellow Flags

Behaviors or characteristics that we might want to pay attention to in a relationship are called yellow flags. They are not necessarily deal breakers, but yellow flags can be a general warning sign that something bigger is going on, or a hint that a red flag – a sign the relationship is bound to end – is close behind. The trick is to acknowledge the yellow flags and tread carefully.

In 1994, Steve and I bought a beautiful 3,500 square foot home in Danville, California. It was on an acre and a half and had a dream view. We bought the home in anticipation of starting a family, but it took both of our incomes to qualify for the loan and we both contributed to the mortgage payment.

A month later is when the interest rates shot up and both of our businesses tanked. It was the first time I experienced a business problem that I had no control over. The speed of the economic impact on our businesses was shocking. Each of us spent the next few years re-building our companies, which meant I was commuting between Phoenix and California every week.

Steve and his partner sold their business as soon as they could. At the time, I was still rebuilding RMCR. I was covering all the expenses of living part-time in Phoenix and half the expenses in California, so I asked him to cover all the bills in California for a few months.

"I didn't sell my business for *us* to live on it," he responded. "Actually, I am going to take a year off of working."

His response surprised me, because first, there was plenty of money to cover a few months without leaving him struggling. Second, this was the first time I heard about him taking a year off. It was a yellow flag I should have paid attention to. He didn't want to help me out by paying for our living expenses in California. And he made a decision about a big life change without talking with me about it?

"What are you planning to do?" I asked, hoping he might say he would come work with me to build our family business.

"I am going to go see my friends, do some traveling and take time off," he replied. "I may never get to do this again."

RMCR was having some challenges, so we both knew there was no way for me to travel with him…even if he invited me, which he didn't – another yellow flag. I asked him to come see me in Phoenix during his time off, thinking about how much fun we had when he visited me in Phoenix before we were married.

"I really do not want to do that," he said.

His responses were hurtful to me. He didn't want to help me in a business that was still bringing in very good money for the family, nor did he want to come to Phoenix to just be with me. My heart told me that was *another* yellow flag.

Since we first met, my head had been telling me that Steve was smarter than me because he went to college and I didn't; he was better than me because he never used drugs, and I did; he could fly helicopters, and on and on. Like an old recording going off in my head, it kept telling me that my own substantial accomplishments in life paled in comparison to his. It would take me a few more hits to my self-confidence before I would realize my own self-worth.

In the meantime, I focused on growing both my business, paid my part of the expenses, and just let Steve do his thing.

Eventually, Steve did make an appearance in Phoenix…when I gave birth to Cole in 1998. Two months after Cole was born, offers started coming in for RMCR.

Don't Tell Me I Can't

Steve and I were over the moon excited about our new baby, Cole. He was the most important part of my being, which made me definitely committed to my new life in California. I had been sober almost a decade and couldn't believe the changes in my life and how great it was. I was so grateful for my sobriety…still am.

When Cole was 10 days old, he and I joined Steve in Danville. After settling in from the move, getting Cole on a schedule, and furnishing the house, I continued commuting to work with RMCR. I would leave on Tuesday evening and return on Thursday night. I hired Becky, a wonderful nanny, and sometimes she would travel with us.

After about six more months, RMCR was thriving again, and I was fortunate to be able to choose from several offers to sell the company. It sold for a nice profit, and I stayed on for a couple of months to help with the transition. Once that sale closed, I gave away or sold everything in Phoenix, including my house.

When Steve and I married, we kept our own checking accounts and paid for the house expenses in a joint account. When the sale of my business and house in Phoenix was finalized, Steve had plans of what we should do with the money. I thought, "Do you have a mouse in your pocket? What is this we?" Since he would not cover California expenses when he sold his business, I was surprised he now wanted to decide what to do with the money from the sale of my business. The yellow flags just kept on coming…

Steve was supposed to be taking a year off from work. He had not been very happy with the work at his last company, and I was hoping his next career would be something that he really enjoyed. He loved flying helicopters, so I encouraged him to become a flight instructor or work in an industry that needed helicopter pilots. He was averse to doing anything that required a risk. I think he felt so much responsibility for supporting a family that he just couldn't bring himself to do anything risky. Instead, he started a background checks company with his former business partner.

Steve and his partner became preoccupied trying to get their new company started. His partner's expertise was in the technical side of the business and Steve's was in operations. So, sales were not coming in like they were anticipating. They were in desperate need of a salesperson, which happened to be in my wheelhouse.

Since background checks was my idea to begin with, Steve asked me to help them out with sales. My non-compete from the sale of my company did not include background checks so I could. I still had this dream of building an empire with him, so I agreed. I was given a desk, a phone and strict instructions that I needed to stay in my lane and not make any decisions about sales, strategy or pricing on my own. It made my eyes roll. Each morning, I took care of Cole's needs, handed him over to Becky, then set out for Steve's office, with a large, iced tea. I diligently sat at the desk, making cold calls.

As much as I love seeing how I can help companies with their business, and closing deals, this was an odd position for me. After years of running my own business, at Steve's company I had no power to make any decisions. Several times I made suggestions on how we could hammer out new deals with potential new clients and my ideas were shut down. No wonder sales are lagging. I was unpleasantly surprised that any creative ideas for closing new business were dismissed without much consideration. It was offensive to me, since their company was built on my original concept.

On top of that, when I asked the staff to do something, they went to Steve, and he told them they didn't have to do what I asked. In spite of the limitations and lack of respect and decision-making ability, I was still able to grow their revenues by 30% in the months I was there. And I could see much more potential, if I had the freedom to make deals.

Finally, I told Steve that I was happy to help, but I wanted to be a partner in the company and run sales. He said he had to talk to his partner about it. Months went by and I continued closing deals and bringing in more revenue.

Periodically, I asked Steve if they were going to make me a partner and his response was his promise that he would follow up with his partner. After expressing my frustration with the false promises, he set up a meeting with the three of us, so they could tell me NO. Dazed, I took the rest of the day off.

At home later, Steve told me his partner and his wife didn't want to give up any of their shares in the company, and that I already had half of Steve's interest, so I should continue to come in and do sales for them based on that. He also asked why I couldn't be happy just being a housewife and stay-at-home-mom, like his partner's wife, and just help out with their business. His partner's wife had no plans to come in and work on their business.

They were happy with the added revenue I'd brought in, but he wanted me to be a housewife and stay home with kids? As much as I adored Cole and wanted another child, I wondered if my husband even knew who he married.

Again, I suggested that we build a new company together. He said he was committed to doing this new business with his partner. I wondered if he made that commitment in front of a priest and family and friends, like when he made the commitment to me.

I realize I put him in the position of having to choose between his wife and his business partner/friend. He chose his business partner. Not me. That's all I heard.

His choice felt deeply personal, like I was being stabbed in the heart. I had sold my company, given birth to our son, I either sold or moved everything I owned to California to build a life with this person who didn't choose me. It hurt, not just on a business level – I knew I had the skills and talent to make their sales fly – but why did I attach myself, financially, physically, and spiritually, to a man who preferred to build with someone else?

It's times like that when good girlfriends are worth more than hundreds of hours in therapy. While crying over it with a good friend, Marjory, she told me if that door did not open, it was because God wants you to open another one. Another girlfriend, Tracey said if her husband did that, she would just compete and kick their ass. I quit crying and set out to build my own damn empire.

The next week, I met with Steve and his partner to tell them that I was fine with their decision to exclude me as a partner. I told them I was no longer going to work for their company as of that day. I was going to go across the street, work out of a closet, use toilet paper for marketing and kick their ass. As some sort of act of contrition, they offered to pay commission for the clients that I brought to them. I told them they could consider my commission a gift and if they didn't pull their business out of the red soon, their clients would know where I'd be.

While trying to reason with me later at home, Steve told me that I could never open a competing business by myself; I wouldn't be able to do it. I told him it was already in the works, and it would be called Private Eyes.

"You will *never* get that name," he scoffed. "I'm sure it's already taken."

The next morning, I drove into San Francisco for the first time in my life and found a parking space right in front of the office of the Secretary of State. Ten minutes later, Private Eyes was a corporation.

We opened on September 2, 1999, and Private Eyes was profitable in its first month.

Don't tell me I can't.

The Launch of Private Eyes

Fueled by disappointment and funds from the sale of RMCR, I quickly found a small office space not far from Steve's office, in Walnut Creek, California. My new first employee turned out to be Amy, an employee of Steve's who found out I was starting my own company and wanted to be a part of it. She became Private Eyes' first employee, and there was an air of expectancy and excitement as we set up the tiny new office.

Those first few weeks were crazy and while I focused on sales, Amy helped with sales *and* operations. We lost no time as we began making sales calls as soon as we got phone lines.

Months earlier, I had contacted the sales division of a large company while working for Steve. I connected with Pamela, who was in the human resources department. We got along great, and she had been interested in background checks, but wasn't ready to sign a contract. Once the office was set up, she was one of the first sales calls I made. Shortly after, she became Private Eyes' first client.

After a couple of months, Pamela was so happy with our service that we were referred to the parent company, the largest wine producer in the world. They started using us as a backup, but we soon became its primary company for background checks. We still serve that business today. It is one of our longest relationships and one I am very proud of.

As both of our companies have grown more than two decades together, we have been able to continue to meet their challenges and changing needs.

We added more clients and brought on more staff as Private Eyes increased revenue.

On the home front, I was about to give birth to our second son, Adam. Steve and I were thrilled to be adding to our family and Cole seemed to be excited about having a baby brother, although I doubt, he understood exactly what that meant. While everything seemed to be going well on the surface, I noticed that Steve and I got along much better back when I was commuting to and from Phoenix.

Or, in other words, when we weren't under the same roof three or four days out of the week.

<hr />

Listen to Your Heart,
Not Your Husband

On September 11, 2001, everything changed. The entire nation watched as our country came under attack. We were all shocked, and then suffered aftershocks as businesses stopped hiring out of fear for the future. We, of course, felt those aftershocks deeply and I had to make changes quickly to the Private Eyes staff while we absorbed the tragedy.

At home, Adam and I were wrestling with his sleep schedule. I was so tired that year because he did not sleep all night, so I was getting up in the middle of the night to feed him and going to work early. I was sleep deprived and overworked…not a good combination.

While talking to a friend who is a former military chaplain, I asked if he had any suggestions on how I could balance work and home responsibilities better. He suggested finding one big client that would bring in enough money to hire people back and lessen my load in the office.

"No big client is going to hire me," I muttered. "I only have five employees; I am a small business."

He told me that God governed every event of my career, and He would figure it out. All I had to do was stay open to the idea and respond when it came to fruition. I figured I had nothing to lose, and it wouldn't cost me anything to just stay open to the idea. So, I did. Every morning as I went into the office, I acknowledged that God would bring me whatever I needed.

In November of 2001, I received the first request for proposal (RFP) I had ever received. It came from Coca-Cola Enterprises. Kaye, Coca-Cola's procurement person, had emailed the RFP to me, she and I connected immediately over the phone. The proposal was due in December.

I could barely contain my excitement when I went home that evening, partly because it was amazing a huge corporation like Coca Cola even had Private Eyes on its radar; partly because it was an answer to my prayer, which meant maybe I was on God's radar, too. And who doesn't want that?

Practically floating into the house, I told Steve about the RFP and my great phone call with Kaye. His response was, "You'll never get it. Your company is not big enough to handle them and now we have two children at home. You just can't do it."

While I was getting used to being told by my husband that I couldn't do something, I was crushed. I thought my spouse should be my biggest cheerleader. If he wasn't capable of being a cheerleader, at least he should refrain from throwing a wet blanket on me…or even worse, verbalizing my own fears that were already staking out space in my head.

That evening, I tossed and turned in bed, wondering if I was taking on more than I could do, more than my small staff could do. Steve's words burned in my mind and made me angry. I would *never* say that to him, if he received a large RFP. I had been supportive of whatever he chose to do from the first day I met him.

Logistically, I was afraid he might be right. We were a small company and getting this client would require an immediate expansion of staff, space, and hours. Adam still wasn't sleeping through the night, and I was the parent who was getting up with him.

On the other hand, this was exactly the anchor client I was praying for. In my heart, I believed that God brought this client to Private Eyes. We had been referred to Coca-Cola's corporate office by a woman we had been working with in the Oakland division. Corporate wanted to standardize procedures nationwide and she had been impressed with our local work. In the wee hours of the morning, when I had to get up with Adam, I finally made the decision to listen to my heart, which was telling me to go for it.

The next few weeks, my team of five divided our time between preparing a proposal for Coca Cola, servicing the clients we already had, and continuing to make sales calls. When we had a final version of the proposal, we attached a magnifying glass to each copy, which highlighted Private Eyes, and we sent them by Federal Express.

We were selected as one of five finalists out of 28 companies, and we were invited to travel to the corporate office in Atlanta to present our plan.

———•◦•———

Hustle & Heart Sets You Apart

Armed with a presentation, Heather and I traveled to Atlanta to meet with Coca-Cola. Heather was the Assistant Director of the San Francisco Opera but was working with me to earn extra money. Opera is her passion. I also arranged for a vendor from Philadelphia who did drug screening to meet us there, since Coca-Cola needed that service, as well.

We were awakened the morning of the presentation by a very loud fire alarm in the hotel. Embassy Suites was on fire and everyone was evacuated. Of course, I grabbed my laptop, which contained the presentation. As I was running down the stairs with other guests of the hotel, I was thinking this isn't a good way to start the day, and if we don't get back into our rooms soon, what am I going to do with my hair?

It didn't take long to put the fire out and we were able to return to our rooms. Since we were scheduled as the last presentation, we had time to go over everything again…and I had time to do my hair!

I began our presentation by thanking the team at Coca-Cola for inviting us there to present because, even though our hotel caught on fire and woke us up that morning, that night was the first time in 14 months I had slept eight consecutive hours because my baby didn't sleep. They all laughed; it was a good start. I also shared Ghirardelli chocolate from the San Francisco Bay Area to give them a taste of California. The meeting was amazing, and we had a great connection. Heather ended the meeting by promising if they selected Private Eyes, she would sing *Phantom of the Opera* at the onboarding meeting. I suspect that may have sealed the deal.

We left Atlanta feeling great. Whether we won the account or not, we had given it our best shot and had a lot of fun meeting with them.

Coca-Cola contacted me within the week to let us know that Private Eyes had been chosen! It felt like magic. They gave us a contract for background checks, drug screening, physicals, and driver qualification file maintenance for all of Coca-Cola Enterprises. I was so excited when I got home from work, anticipating a big celebration with the news.

"Guess what?" I said to Steve, with a big smile on my face. "We WON the Coca-Cola account. All of it." I was expecting a big hug and congratulations.

"Tell them you will take half," Steve responded, without any congratulations. "You cannot handle it all."

"They don't want a company to do half, they want someone to do all of it," I said. "And Private Eyes is the company to do it ALL!" I had to leave the room and go call friends who would be more excited about the news, since my husband couldn't be.

The next step was for Coca-Cola to conduct on an onsite inspection of Private Eyes office, as well as the drug screening vendor in Philadelphia. Again, we had an awesome meeting with the Coca-Cola team. We decorated our offices with Coca-Cola signs and swag to welcome them and we ended the day at dinner at Boulevard in San Francisco.

Next, it was time to make the trip to Philadelphia for our vendor's onsite inspection.

Is Pepsi OK?

With one onsite inspection under our belts, our next step was to do an inspection in Philadelphia with the vendor I had chosen for the drug screening, physicals and driver qualification file maintenance. So far, I had been communicating with the sales representative to negotiate their services and make arrangements for the onsite inspection, but the owner of the company wanted to meet me personally, now that Coca-Cola was coming to his office and I had the contract. Before that, he was not interested in meeting me. He asked me to come a day early so we could meet each other and talk, and he picked me up at the airport.

His office was in a high rise building and he asked me to wait in the conference room, while he gathered paperwork. When he returned, he placed a non-disclosure agreement (NDA) in front of me and asked me to sign it. Under the NDA was a new contract, stating Coca-Cola Enterprises would pay him and he would then pay Private Eyes, essentially making Coca-Cola his client, rather than Private Eyes. He reasoned that his company was larger, therefore, the money should go through them. To add insult upon insult, he added a petty comment that the boots I was wearing were evidence that I could not have as much money as he did.

"I'm not going to sign anything without my attorney reviewing it," I responded, ignoring his crappy I've-got-more-money-than-you comment.

"Then you will not be able to be in the meeting tomorrow," he said.

I left his office and checked into my hotel. I then called Kaye at Coca-Cola on her mobile phone and told her what happened. I was so disappointed by what had happened and while explaining it to her, I started to cry. Then, I was completely embarrassed.

"Our team is already here," she said. "So, let's go to the meeting tomorrow and see what happens." I didn't sleep much, reliving the contentious meeting with the vendor. I thought of a million things I wish I would have said to him but didn't.

We all gathered in the vendor's conference room the following morning. He started the meeting.

"Sandra cannot be in the room because she did not sign our NDA," he said to everyone. "So, I'm going to escort her to the lobby."

I had no idea what was going to happen, but I had decided that contrary to what I felt like doing, I was going to be gracious. I rose from my seat at the large table and walked to the door. Silently, he walked me to the lobby, where I sat for the entire morning. I kept reminding myself that if God had brought me this client, then nothing would stand in the way. I tried to occupy my thoughts by doing some work while I waited.

A little before noon, everyone came out of the conference room to go to lunch. The vendor had made reservations at a private club in the high rise building next door. Lunch had its problems. First, there was some fierce negotiating with the maître' d over the fact that Mike, Coca-Cola's Security Manager, was wearing a Coca-Cola polo shirt and had no jacket, and at this club, jackets were required for men. Once that was settled, the bigger problem presented itself.

As we ordered lunch Kaye asked for a Diet Coke.

"We don't carry Coke products," the server said. "Is Pepsi okay?"

If I hadn't already decided I wasn't going to work with this vendor, I would have been angry that he didn't have someone in his *large company* check to make sure where we were dining served the client's products. As it was, I enjoyed the embarrassment he clearly felt. Kaye, of course, emphatically declined Pepsi.

Before going back into the conference room after lunch, the women all went to the lady's room.

"When we go back into the conference room, we will be talking about pricing and billing," said MeLinda, Coca-Cola's HR Manager. "So, you are coming in the room this afternoon."

As we all took our seats in the conference room, the vendor repeated that I couldn't be in the room.

"We are going to talk about pricing, and the billing is going through Private Eyes, so she has to be here," said MeL. "It is her contract."

He turned red as red could be from his neck up and turned to Mike, the only other man in the room. "You understand, don't you," he said. "My company is much bigger than hers." He spread his arms out, asking us to take in the high-rise offices and big conference room as proof of his stability and integrity.

Mike slowly shook his head. "All I know," he said. "Is if you do not do what Kaye is asking you to do, you will *never* do business with Coca-Cola."

I thought the vendor was going to explode. He got up and left the room, throwing out his prediction that Coca-Cola would be back after Private Eyes failed them.

We were all stunned and looked at each other. "I guess this meeting's over," Kaye said, clearly not happy. We gathered our things and went to the lobby. The vendor's assistant let us know that she had arranged a car to take us all back to the airport.

As we separated to catch our flights, Kaye said she would be in touch the next day. I had so much anxiety. I was afraid this guy had just blown this once-in-a-lifetime opportunity for Private Eyes. As soon as I returned home, I started searching for a replacement vendor, hoping Coca-Cola might give me another chance.

The next day Kaye called me and said they'd had a meeting and they wanted me to find another vendor. I was so relieved we were on the same page. I told her I was already searching.

"Anyone will work with you now," she said. "You have the Coca-Cola account."

And, just like that, I found another vendor.

Drinking from the Firehose

To start the Coca-Cola account, we needed to onboard the company's 120 recruiters, so they could start using Private Eyes' services. That meeting was scheduled to take place in Dallas. A welcome dinner had been planned for the evening before the day of training.

Once everyone was seated, and we were introduced, I explained to the recruiters that Private Eyes needed to fulfill a promise we had made if we won the Coca-Cola account. Then, Heather stepped up to the microphone and beautifully sang Phantom of the Opera. She received a standing ovation, and we were off to a good start.

As we talked to recruiters throughout the day, a number of them mentioned they sometimes order as many as 10 background checks every day. I am a numbers person, and as I started adding up the possible reports that might start coming in, panic started toying with me. In Coca-Cola's RFP, it said to expect approximately 7,000 background checks per year, which might be around 25 reports each day, total. At the time, they were not standardized, so it was an approximation. Even with that number, I knew I was going to have to scale up quickly.

The Coca-Cola account turned out to be much larger than any of us had thought, including all the HR executives. The recruiters ended up ordering more than 30,000 background checks, 30,000 drug tests and other services from us in the first year. It felt like we were drinking from the firehose, and summer, Coca-Cola's busiest season, was looming in front of us.

In a meeting with Coca-Cola in April, we talked about the unanticipated volume of reports coming in. They agreed to slow down the onboarding by having their largest divisions back off. We agreed that would give Private Eyes time to expand our operations. They told me if I could get everything working with all of their divisions, the Coca-Cola account would stay with Private Eyes forever; if not, they would leave in September.

I agreed to have offices hours from 5am-5pm PST so any Coca-Cola division could contact Private Eyes during these hours and get a live person. It was an adjustment from the typical 8am-5pm, but I didn't mind the early morning hours -- I was brought up working those kinds of hours on the farm. I had a burning desire to make this work and was willing to do whatever it took. I was hiring and training people as fast as I could.

That summer was a hot one, and the volume of Coca-Cola products being sold was huge. All of the Coca-Cola divisions were hiring as fast as they could, so the volume of background checks was even greater. It was all hands-on deck; even friends of mine came in to help process reports. But not my husband. He refused to help, even though my long hours kept me from being at home.

My friend, John Qualtrough, supported me every day by telling me that I could do it. He even arranged for his friend Chris Wright, an entrepreneur and former CEO, to help me that first summer for free. He wanted me to believe that this was all going to work out, and he kept telling me that God would provide the right people for me to do the job. Chris helped with recruiting employees, and we went from six staff members to 36 within a month.

I was getting up at 3:30 in the morning to get ready to go into the office. I probably could have given myself one more hour of sleep, but I always wanted to have my hair, makeup, and clothes look good because I represented Private Eyes. I still feel that looking my best helps me feel sharp and ready for anything…and anything can happen while you are building a company.

In the beginning of onboarding Coca-Cola, I actually tried to work 5am to 5pm, then go home and cook homemade meals. I also would go to Costco, Target, and the grocery store to get food, diapers, formula, plan meals, and more. Eventually, I could not keep up with everything, so I told Steve that he and the nanny would need to take over the shopping and cooking until summer was over.

As the volume of reports came in, I was working most weekdays until 10pm. By the time I got home, the boys were in bed, so while it was hard to get up at night if Adam or Cole needed something, I cherished the time I got to spend with them in those hours. I also worked weekends when I needed to over that summer. I remember Steve calling me at work one day to tell me we were out of milk. My team and I were trying to get hundreds of reports out the door and he wanted me to run out and get him some milk? I was exasperated and nearly snapped.

"I feel like you are trying to push a boulder up a hill all by yourself," MeL said to me one day. I assured her I was not alone, and that Private Eyes was going to do it.

The summer ended and we survived. Coca-Cola stayed on board and by the end of the year, we had all the divisions utilizing Private Eyes!

A Dark Conversation

About six months into working with Coca-Cola, I came home at 10pm, after being at work since 5am to find Steve sitting in the living room in the dark. He said he needed to talk to me. Any time someone says they need to talk to me; my brain goes on alert. How long had he been sitting in the dark and why didn't he turn on a light? Was this going to be a "dark" conversation? Exhausted, and not really interested in having a heavy conversation, I turned on a light and stood in the doorway.

"What's up?" I said.

"My partner and I had a conversation and we decided that now we will merge with you," he said.

I couldn't believe the arrogance. Now that they saw how big this account was going to be, they wanted in on it? But there was more...

He continued, "You can keep 51 percent to keep that woman-owned thing going."

My brain was about to explode. They had it all figured out. I wondered how many hours at their office they wasted on hammering out this deal. How gracious of them to let me keep 51 percent of a company I built from nothing. And they could benefit from it still being woman-owned!

"If you don't do this, you won't keep Coca-Cola," Steve warned. At this point, I was already scaled up to handle all that Coca-Cola was sending us, things were running relatively smoothly, and money was flowing in.

I had been up since 3:30am that day and I was done. I wanted to kiss my kids and go to sleep. I didn't want to get into a nasty discussion about how hurt I was that he chose working with his business partner over me; that he had been so negative about me being successful; that he didn't even want to help me when I really needed it; and on and on. So, I made my answer short.

"Thanks, but no thanks," I said. "Watch the kids and I will see you in the fall."

I went to bed really angry that night, as I replayed their offer, followed by a warning that I would fail. On one hand, it reminded me how far Private Eyes had come to be able to accommodate a large account – so much so that my husband and his partner now wanted a piece of it. On the other hand, here he was again, telling me I couldn't do something that I obviously already accomplished!

Funny thing was that they didn't even try to come back with a different offer. No wonder they had sales problems. Not that I would consider it, and maybe they sensed that. I was still putting in long hours, but we had gotten through the busiest season, and I expected things to slow down a bit.

This, to me, was a once in a lifetime opportunity that could change the future for our lives and our children.

The burning question that kept repeating in my head was, why couldn't Steve be proud of me and rejoice in the abundance that was coming our way?

Was I still looking to prove my dad wrong about his low expectations of me? Was I looking for his approval? Acceptance? Did my husband have those same low expectations? What had I done...married my dad?

Super Bowl v. Mom's Funeral

In 1998, after Cole was born, my mother was diagnosed with Alzheimer's. It was a difficult adjustment for my dad, but he insisted on caring for her at home with my grandma's help. Two years later, my dad was diagnosed with stage 4 colon cancer. He juggled aggressive treatment, surgery, chemo, and radiation while taking care of my mom. In November of 2002 he called me on a Wednesday.

"I am done," he said. "I am going to start taking morphine Friday."

Two weeks before that call, Adam, Cole, and I had traveled with my friend, Madeline, to Nebraska so my dad could see the boys. It was a little chaotic and I was no help with my mom because I was chasing the boys around the entire time. While we were there, Madeline gave my dad and grandma a massage – the first either had experienced. Afterward, my dad came upstairs.

"Now I know why you have always asked me to get a massage," sighed Dad. "That was great." He sat next to me on the fireplace hearth.

"You are a good kid and you made two perfect boys," he said. "I am so proud of you and how you won the Coca-Cola account. Your husband couldn't do that; only you did that."

"Thank you, Dad," I replied. "You know, I got my work ethic from you."

"Well, I'm proud of you and I love you," he said.

I think that is the only time in my life he ever said that to me.

When I arrived on the Friday that Dad was planning to start checking out, most of my siblings and their spouses were at our parents' house. My heart broke when I saw my dad. He looked so different from when I saw him only two weeks prior. The cancer had spread to his lungs, and he coughed constantly. The disease and the caring of mom had really taken its toll on him, and I had to focus to keep from crying at the sight of his weakened body. Although I no longer answered to him, this was the man who I had tried to please my whole life. He reigned huge in my mind and the realization that his life was about to end was crushing.

"This is a bunch of shit and I'm done," he announced to everyone in the room. "Please take care of your mom and don't put her in a home." We all promised we wouldn't put mom in a home, although there wasn't a plan in place yet for taking care of her.

My dad passed away on that Sunday. He woke up right before passing and asked if we all had work. Then he said he hoped all the stuff I had been saying to him about passing to the other side was true. My siblings and I all laughed. Then he asked if Duke, my youngest brother, the baby of the family, had work. Clearly, it was important for him to know that we all had jobs and an income. We assured him that we were all taken care of. Shortly after hearing that, he passed.

Dad had a few stipulations for his burial. He wanted to be buried the day after he died, in his cowboy boots, and only have our mom and the kids at his funeral.

"Nobody helped me all these years," he said. "If they did not see me when I was alive, they do not need to see me when I am dead."

When I called Steve to let him know Dad had passed, he offered to catch a flight to Nebraska, but I told him not to because the service was scheduled for the next day, and I would be on a flight back to California immediately afterward. When I flew back to Oakland and drove home, it was about 10pm and everyone was in bed sleeping. I was upset that Steve didn't stay up to console or talk to me. The next morning, I took care of the boys and went to work without talking to my husband.

The next day, my siblings called to tell me they were putting my mom in a home. I was devastated, I screamed and yelled and went ballistic. Dad had asked me specifically not to do that and we had all finally agreed on taking turns with a week at a time staying with her. However, they had devised a different plan and waited for me to leave to implement it.

When they called me, I was in Cole's room with him, and I could not control my emotions. I cried and cried hysterically, even though I understood it was the best thing to do. Steve came back from a run with Adam and looked at me sobbing on the floor in Cole's room and turned around and walked away. I always wondered why he never tried to console me or talk to me about what was wrong. I felt so alone and could have really used a hug, at least.

A couple of months after my dad passed, mom had a heart attack and even though she had a DNR, the memory-loss home where she was living called 911. After she was resuscitated, my sister, Annette, picked her up at the hospital.

"I am ready to go and be with the Lord," Mom said.

Annette called all of us and we headed back to Nebraska. Mom passed away soon after everyone gathered. I called Steve and asked him to fly out with the boys for the funeral. Having them attend the funeral wasn't as important to me as the feeling that I wanted them with me. Losing both parents within three months of each other broke my heart.

I needed to hold my boys and feel their arms around me. I needed the same from Steve.

"What about the Super Bowl party we have planned for tomorrow?" Steve asked. The Super Bowl was the last thing I wanted to think about. We had invited a few close friends over to watch the Super Bowl. It had been planned for more than a month.

"CANCEL IT!" is what I wanted to scream over the telephone. I was annoyed that he even considered a Super Bowl party as a factor in this situation. I was even more annoyed that he couldn't come up with a solution on his own. Clearly, I was on my last nerve.

"I guess if you don't want to cancel it, you could catch a 6am flight with the boys or, have the nanny keep the boys and come by yourself," I replied, as calmly as I could muster. "If you fly out early enough, you can get here just in time for the funeral, then we can go home."

"I really don't want to do that," he said. That was the end of the conversation.

Steve did not come to my mom's funeral; instead, he hosted his Super Bowl party at our house in California without me. When I returned home the next evening, I walked into a dark, silent house. Again, Steve hadn't stayed up for me. This time, I felt more angry than hurt that Steve didn't care enough to join me for my mom's funeral or at least wait up for me when I got home.

A week after I arrived back home, I was at the grocery store and ran into a woman that was at my house for the Super Bowl party and she asked why I wasn't there for the big game.

"I was at my mom's funeral," I replied.

"Oh, I'm so sorry. I did not know," she said, horrified.

Did Steve really have a Super Bowl party and not tell "our friends" that I had just lost my mom? Didn't they wonder where I was and if so, what *did* Steve tell them?

All the yellow flags that had been piling up in this marriage were turning red.

———◆◆———

Can't You Just Do It?

Coming home after my mom's funeral, I didn't know what to do about my marriage. Steve not coming to the funeral felt like the last straw. I was angry and I felt like I was starting to look like an angry woman. My favorite saying at the time and at work was "Life is good" but my face was not looking like that was a true statement. My anger was showing.

The day I got back from the funeral, five corporate executives from Coca-Cola landed in California to visit my office for a few days. I had plans for dinner with them at least one night, maybe two. After they arrived, Steve told me he was going to his good friend Kelvyn's 40th birthday party in Seattle. He left with no notice or help to find support to take care of the boys while my largest client was in town. He must have been quietly planning this trip while I was attending mom's funeral.

When he returned, I told him we needed to go to counseling. He agreed to go. The counselor told Steve that he needed to pursue me because relationships always work better when the man does the pursuing. Plus, he said we need to make some new good memories so we can replace some of the bad ones we were focusing on.

We left the meeting and Steve asked me to go to lunch at Subway. We talked about what the counselor told us and the part where he suggested that Steve needed to be more aggressive in pursuing me.

"Can't you just do it?" he asked.

"What? Pursue myself?" I responded. Or was I supposed to pursue Steve? I was amazed he asked that.

Eventually, after a couple of meetings, the counselor said, "I do not know why, but Steve really does not want to do it."

I decided if we separated, then maybe Steve would realize what he had with me, and he would fight for our marriage and our life together. On paper, we had a great life: two healthy, active boys, a beautiful home, successful businesses, healthy bank accounts, and a very positive financial outlook. We used to have a lot of fun together and even though it was clear we wouldn't be building a family business together, the future looked very good. I thought he would be miserable and pursue me to keep what we had and keep the family together.

I thought wrong.

———◆———

Baby Grand Piano

In October of 2004 after much counseling and no improvements Steve and I agreed to separate. I stayed in our house with the boys, and he moved to a townhouse in a neighboring community. I was surprised to learn that he had already researched alternative housing and was ready to make the move.

Regardless of his planning ahead, I think it was more difficult to let go than he anticipated. He kept showing up at the house unannounced, sometimes scaring the daylights out of me. Often, when I put the boys to bed, I fell asleep reading to them. Several times, when I woke up and walked around the house turning off lights for the night, checking door and window locks and making sure everything was turned off, I would find Steve sitting in the dark in the living room! The first time that happened, I froze and nearly had a heart attack; as it happened more often, it became awkward and uncomfortable. He wasn't there to see or talk to me and the boys didn't know he was there. I'm not sure why he was silently entering the house and just sitting there in the dark.

That situation prompted me to go see him (during daylight hours) and try to settle the details of our divorce and move forward. I made my list of how I thought we could divide everything fairly, because it's always good to have in mind your needs versus your wants when you start negotiations. Needs are non-negotiable; wants can be negotiated.

I started our negotiations by suggesting maybe we would be better neighbors and friends, than husband and wife. On the list of things, I would give up was the house and furnishings, his 1969 Jaguar, his Airforce retirement and 401K account, his business, and other items that I knew were important to him. I just wanted cash so I could buy a house in the neighborhood, so we could both see the boys every day. He agreed, and I will forever be grateful for that particular discussion going so smoothly.

A few months later, I bought a $1.2 million dollar house around the corner from our original home. The location was perfect. It would make it convenient for the boys to walk or ride their bikes to their dad's house and both of us could see the boys daily, as they grew. My clothes, the boys' clothes, a guest room bed and the baby grand piano were the only items I took from our house. I bought all new furniture, kitchen items, and bedroom furniture for the boys with a home equity loan. Steve moved back into our original house, and we began what would be our new normal life.

As I settled into my new home, I still had hopes Steve would come to his senses and miss the life we had built together. We had so much in terms of what our society calls success; we just didn't get along. It broke my heart that we split up. About a week later, I went to see Steve to see if he missed me and the life we had. He had already replaced the baby grand piano!

Suddenly, it hit me. He was done with our marriage a long time ago and he just didn't have the guts to pull the trigger. But once it was pulled, it must have also triggered his anger, because the divorce suddenly became nasty.

Shortly after I realized our marriage was truly over, I was served papers that he filed for divorce. Later, I was served more papers saying he not only wanted all the assets I had already agreed to, but he also wanted part of Private Eyes to complete the settlement of divorce. I wouldn't even consider it and replied with a hard NO.

I told him, "We can fight over things all day long, but what you don't realize is that *I am* the asset."

We battled back and forth over this for a long time, so the divorce was not finalized for years.

He also took me to court asking for full custody of the boys because he claimed I worked all the time. I thought it was absurd that he was asking for more money from me *and* that the boys should be taken from me because I was earning the money he wanted. He also went to the Catholic Church to get an annulment of our marriage, claiming in the paperwork that I was an addict as his reason. After more than a decade of sobriety, two children, and a successful business, he was throwing that out there as grounds for pretending we never married. I couldn't believe he was trying to erase everything we had done together.

Fortunately, my siblings, friends, and business associates who know me wrote letters stating that we were married in the Catholic Church, and we agreed to have children and consummated them. I admitted I was an addict in recovery, but I was sober more than 10 years before I had children, and I was sober when I got married and pregnant. The Catholic Church denied his request.

Steve's hostility toward me made the first year of our divorce brutal, not only for me, but for the kids, as well. I'd like to say I always took the high road but looking back, I was very angry. One morning, I was getting the boys in the car to take them to school and Steve pulled into my driveway blocking my car.

"I am taking them to school," I told him, as I pointed to the kids buckled into the car seats. "We are all ready to go."

"No!" he growled, as he tried to pull the boys out of the car to go with him.

I tried to stop him, and the boys started crying. He left us all crying in the driveway. We argued over taking the boys to school??? I probably should have just let him take them. At least the boys wouldn't have started their day crying over an argument their parents had in the driveway. It was a frustrating time.

Later that night, after I put Adam to bed, Cole and I were sitting on the floor in the kitchen, talking.

"Mom, I know you are going to be okay," he said. "I do not know if dad will be."

We were both crying by now.

I hugged him and told him we would all be okay. His comment gave me a little more compassion for Steve and what he might be feeling during this first year of divorce.

———◆———

Life Changes

Life was settling down after the divorce, although my lawyers and I were still fending off my ex-husband's grab at Private Eyes. The business was running smoothly, the Coca-Cola account was doing well, and we had added some smaller clients. I understood why Steve wanted a part of it -- Private Eyes was going gangbusters and losing my financial contribution to his lifestyle made him nervous.

The boys and I had hit a groove, with the help of a nanny. I missed them when they spent time with Steve, but they loved their dad, and I was happy to see him continuing an active role in their lives. I know sometimes that's not the case, so I have always been grateful for that. I was really trying to forgive Steve and move on to have a healthy relationship with him for my boys.

I was also learning how to be on my own. Although I was open to be in a new romantic relationship, I had found a calmness and satisfaction being single again. I regularly attended a hot yoga class, joined a business organization, and became comfortable dining by myself.

Bank deposits for Private Eyes became one of my favorite parts of the day. I wasn't doing electronic deposits yet, so I would take a break from the office, go make a deposit and then walk over to my favorite restaurant for lunch by myself. Often, I was seated in the same section, which was overseen by a server named Martín. He learned my order right away because I ordered the same thing every time: an iced tea, bread, a cup of soup or salad. He was always kind to me, and he was very handsome, so I started asking for his table all the time. For years I was a regular customer.

Martín and I became friends and when the restaurant was slow, we talked about our lives. I told him when the boys were with Steve, I missed them terribly. I was not looking forward to spending my first Christmas without them. The two previous holidays we had spent together trying to make it easier on the boys, but that year, Steve was taking them to Sacramento to see their uncle and cousins. I told Martín that even working longer hours couldn't shake the empty feeling that enveloped me this holiday season.

On Christmas Eve day, the telephone rang. I had just returned home from a hot yoga class, and I answered the phone hoping it was one of the boys or Steve, letting me know when they would be returning. I had no idea when to expect them.

It was Martín on the phone. "How is your heart?" he asked. I started to cry.

Martín asked if I would meet him at Peet's coffee house in Walnut Creek. He said he had something for me. Relieved to have a distraction from my empty house, I agreed.

It felt a little odd meeting Martín outside of the restaurant. It was the first time that I had ever seen him not in his restaurant uniform, like when you run into your teacher outside of high school and are reminded that they actually have a life separate from the classroom.

He looked great. He was wearing jeans, a white tee shirt and red sneakers. He looked great...did I already say that?

We ordered coffee, then Martín pulled out a frame with photos of sunsets and sunrises.

"You changed my life," he said. "I want to give this to you as a thank you."

He was referring to the time he had hurt his back and doctors had told him he would not run or box again. I had told him about *Dreamer*, a movie I had just watched with my kids. The movie was inspired by the true story of a horse that was in an accident and broke its leg. Veterinarians had told the owners that the horse would never race again, but their daughter nursed Dreamer back to health. The horse healed and went on to win an important race.

"If Dreamer can race and win, then you can run and box," I had told him. "Just get started."

And he did. He wanted to let me know that he was boxing professionally, swimming and running again.

When we left Peet's, Martín gave me a hug and I felt sparks in my stomach.

Later, Martín returned the favor when he introduced me to his friends, Rich and Yvonne. The couple owned Challenge Day, an organization that helps young people and adults learn to connect through powerful, life-changing programs in schools and communities. Challenge Day does incredible work and was featured on *Oprah* in 2006. Rich and Yvonne gave me a weekend course, called Be the Change. I participated in the program at the beginning of December 2006, and it really opened my heart. I believe that was the beginning of healing my relationship with my ex-husband.

Spinning Plates

As a child, I loved watching the plate spinner on The Ed Sullivan Show. He would get one glass plate spinning on the tip of a stick, then add another stick and plate, and another, until he had about five plates spinning. When a plate would start wobbling, he ran over to the stick and twirled it to keep the plate from falling off the stick. It was frantic and he was moving from stick to stick quickly.

Being an entrepreneur, sometimes I feel like a plate spinner, trying to keep everything spinning, so nothing falls to the ground. Add in the single parent component, and at times, my life required the balancing and flexibility skills that seem to rival Cirque du Soleil!

My life was full. In 2007, even though the divorce still was not final, we had been living in the house I bought for three years, and our lives had settled into a comfortable rhythm. While it had been fun hanging out with Martín, I could see our friendship was getting to be more serious. It seemed that he had been asking me to do things for months now whenever the boys were with their dad. We hiked, met for tea, had dinners together, took walks in the park, sat at the park talking, and took in an occasional movie. We shared personal triumphs and losses; we cried together over him losing his grandfather when he was young, and the pain from my divorce. Then, we would laugh so hard that our stomachs hurt. Soon I felt that he was my best friend and I loved him.

It had been months and nothing romantic had happened; we were just there for each other, and a strong friendship had developed.

However, even though I felt a huge loneliness since the divorce, I had a list of very good reasons we shouldn't see each other anymore. First of all, I was at the voluntary beck and call of my boys; I was busy with Private Eyes; Martín was from Mexico, and we were from very different backgrounds; he was much younger; and I was mortified that I might be considered a "cougar." I brought all of this up when he asked me to meet him one Saturday morning.

"I felt like I was getting ready for a date today," I explained. "This isn't okay because there is too big a gap in our ages for us to date. I also need to think about my boys first."

"So, we just aren't going to hang out or be friends anymore? That's just it?" he asked.

"Yes, I think that is best," I replied, although it made me sad to say it aloud.

"Well, that's too bad, because I wanted to show you something today," he said. "And what are you going to do if you are not going to hang out with me? You do not have the boys today."

"I have to go to Costco, and I will go do my hot yoga class again," I replied, defensively. Bikram Hot Yoga was something I started doing when Steve and I separated and was doing it at least five times per week by then. It had made me lean and sane, and it was something I came to depend upon to help me manage my anger and disappointment. It helped me become, and to stay, optimistic, calm, and grateful.

"But I had the whole day planned," Martín said. "Please go with me today and if, at the end of the day, you feel the same way then we will be done." I agreed to go.

Our first stop was at the Redwood Forest, where we hiked through the beautiful trees. It was raining lightly when we went back to the car, and he picked me up and put me on his shoulders to get me back to my car without getting my shoes muddy. Following the hike, we dined at a waterfront Mexican restaurant in Tiburon, which overlooked the San Francisco Bay.

We drove over the Golden Gate Bridge to visit a museum, then we went to see *The Mexican* at the Metreon Center in San Francisco. We ended the day at nearly midnight back at Peet's Coffeehouse, where we had started.

It was an amazing day! When he kissed me goodbye, he lightly bit my lip, and I knew I was crazy about him. As I was lying in bed that night, completely unable to sleep, he called me and asked what I was doing. I told him I was meditating. He laughed – the laugh of a man who knew he'd conquered my heart.

When the boys were with their dad, Martín and I spent more time together and every time he saw me, he brought me flowers. It was so endearingly sweet. I always brought them home and put them in water on the kitchen counter.

"Mom where are all these flowers coming from?" asked Cole, my oldest son, who was seven years old, going on 30.

"Martín," I replied.

"Who is he?" he asked. I hadn't introduced the boys to Martín yet. Telling them I was dating someone made me nervous for several reasons. What if they didn't like Martín? What if they didn't like the idea of me dating someone? What if Martín and I broke up after the boys became friends with him? The" what ifs" made me hesitant to introduce everyone.

"Martín is a friend of mine," I explained. "When you and Adam are with your dad, sometimes I spend time with him."

"So, Martín keeps giving you flowers?" he asked. "What if I want to meet him?" Cole had always been intuitive and protective of our family.

"I would be happy to have you meet him," I said.

"What if I do not like him?" he asked, squinting his eyes.

I laughed. "Then you will not have to be around him."

At that point, I needed to have another conversation with Martín. I explained to him that if I was going to allow the boys to meet him, he had to know that in our relationship, they would always come first for me. That didn't diminish how I felt about *him*, but the mom in me would always put them first.

"I get it," Martín said. "When they are with you, there is no 'us;' it is all of them."

We set up a day and time for Martín to meet the boys when I took them to the park. He took photos of them and chased them around the park. Of course, anyone who had the energy and was willing to chase them around was welcome in their world. Both boys liked him right away. I imagine Martín slept well that night after playing with them all afternoon.

After that day in the park, everything started to change between us. Martín watched me go back and forth to run Private Eyes, manage a nanny, oversee all the household things, shopping, cooking, laundry, cleaning, schoolwork for the boys, packing lunches, and all the things a single mom has to do. Finally, he sat me down one evening.

"I can help you," he said.

"With what?" I replied, not sure what he was talking about. At this point, I was on autopilot to get things done, so it didn't register with me.

"Everything," he said.

It was a gift I couldn't even wrap my head around, at first. Martín became a strong support of our family and business, keeping our plates spinning. No task was too big or too small; he was willing – actually *enthusiastic* – to spin those plates.

Hard Conversations

"New love! Enjoy it!" Complete strangers would call out to Martín and me when they saw us walking hand-in-hand.

Friends would ask me what I was doing with Martín or what I was going to do with him. I don't know if it was our age difference, our nationality difference, or just the fact that I was dating again that would prompt that question.

"I am going to keep this going as long as I can!" I replied every time, with a big smile on my face. I had never felt so cared for and was amazed Martín's first concern was if Cole, Adam, and I were doing well every day! It felt like a magical dream that I always wanted in a relationship but could never have. This was my new reality, and I was loving it.

A friend of mine, "Tiger" Rebecca Harrison, who is a top realtor in the San Francisco Bay Area, had seen me when I was first separated from Steve at the beginning of our divorce. She witnessed me screaming at my divorce attorney, who hung up on me.

"WTF?" I yelled. "Who does he think he is? He is fired!"

A few years later, she saw me again.

"What happened?" she asked. "You are so different and positive."

"LOVE!" I replied.

Feeling loved was having a huge impact on me and Martín gave me that gift.

One day, Cole asked me, "Why does Martín do all of these things for us mom?"

"I believe he loves us, Cole," I replied, smiling at the thought of it.

"I think he loves *you*," Cole said.

"Cole, he would have to love you and Adam too, to be able to do all he does for us," I said.

Of course, we sometimes got upset but when Martín and I first got together, we made a few agreements. Communication is key to every relationship but making promises to each other that identify specific behaviors that we both wanted to conquer became invaluable down the road. Each admitted that we had both left previous relationships when there was an argument, so we agreed to never leave each other during an argument. We also agreed to recover and make up faster.

It's good to make these kinds of agreements when you are happy and sane. They become touchstones later when things might be less conducive for resolution. We were – and still are -- very happy, thanks to the decision we made years ago to always choose happiness and not stay mad at each other.

Old habits are hard to break though, and one time when I became upset, I got in the car and started driving down the street. Not only is it not a good idea to get behind the wheel of a car when you are angry, but I remembered Martín's and my agreement to never leave. I turned the car around and drove back to the house. After taking a minute by myself in our bedroom, I found Martín to talk to and make up.

An agreement I wanted Martín to sign off on was about being a team player. When my feet hit the ground in the morning, I wanted his to hit the floor, too. I told him I would not be happy with my man staying in bed later than me; I needed a team player who was all in. Many times, Martín was out of bed before me, so he could make everyone breakfast and pack lunches.

Our third agreement was about the boy's taking priority when they were with us. We had already discussed this topic, but I wanted it to be part of our agreement.

Martín and I made a great team and got a groove down very quickly. I went to work at 5am and he got the boys up, got them breakfast, lunches, and snacks ready, and took them to school. He would then meet me at Private Eyes. Eventually, he quit his other jobs and started working with Private Eyes full-time. He did sales calls, and recruitment of new employees, and he was dedicated to helping to build the family business that I'd always dreamed of. Now and then, if he forgot a snack for the boys, he felt terrible and would leave the office and make sure they had what they needed.

When we had the boys, we took turns picking them up after school, helping them with homework, and cooking dinner. It felt so good to have that support and love.

One day, I was looking for an electronic toy of Adam's. Martín had put it away and I was trying to find it when, instead, I found a ring box. I opened it and found a wedding ring. I was shocked. It had been more than three years since Martín and I got together, but now it looked like he was going to ask me to marry him.

After my divorce, I never thought I would ever marry again. I never wanted to upend our lives or divide up everything I owned again. Of course, that's assuming another marriage would end in divorce, but I never thought my marriage to Steve would end in divorce, either.

Besides, I already had kids and I wasn't interested in having more… why would I want to get married?

Realizing Martín wanted to get married freaked me out. I was afraid it would change this great thing we had been doing. I didn't know what I was going to say to him. So, I did the most logical thing I could think of at the time. I picked a fight with him and stayed mad for a couple of days while I thought about almost nothing else.

After a couple of days of near silence between us, Martín walked into my office. I told him I had good news and bad news.

"Give me the good news first," he said.

"I cannot keep a secret from you," I replied.

"And the bad news?" he asked.

"I found the ring," I said, watching his face closely.

"Oh, my god," he exclaimed. "That is why you have been mad? You do not want to marry me? I don't know what I will do if you say no."

He was very upset and said he needed to take a moment. He left my office. That moment turned into days, then weeks. Then surprisingly, weeks turned into months. We were still living together, and everything kept moving along as it had been, but nothing was said about the ring or marriage.

While Martín was taking a moment, I used the time to examine my own fears and resistance to another marriage. In the discussions in my head, I always came to the same bottom line: Martín had captured my heart, and I could no longer imagine life without him. I wanted to be legally married to this man. I felt bad that I had picked a fight and stayed mad; it was not an honest way to handle the situation and I needed to let him know I wanted a marriage proposal from him.

I started to drop hints and tease him about the ring and kept asking him if he was going to ask me or not. I kept it light, and he would always just grin and say nothing.

Finally, one Sunday afternoon we went to Muir Beach. It was one of those beautiful California days, very few clouds in the blue sky and the sun shining off the ocean. He motioned for me to sit on one of the big rocks. Instead of sitting next to me, Martín kneeled on one knee and asked me to marry him.

Of course, I said YES! It was so easy and felt so right. I had no hesitations, but I wondered if we might run into one roadblock.

There was a conversation I needed to have with the love of my life, and it was not a sexy one. It was about a prenuptial agreement. After the initial excitement about our engagement wore down a bit, I approached the subject of a pre-nup. I started the conversation carefully; I didn't want this to turn difficult or ugly, but it had to be done. Clearly Martín had already thought about it, because before I even got the word, pre-nup, out of my mouth, he responded.

"I am a grown ass man," Martín interrupted, as he reached out and took my hands. "If I cannot take care of myself then what am I?"

We had a pre-nup drawn up and signed within the week. It was a lesson to me to go ahead and have the hard conversations…you might be surprised at the response.

Losing 85%

In 2007, I started to get worried. Personnel changes were taking place at Coca-Cola Enterprises and the people I had been working with for over five years were leaving for various reasons. A couple of people were retiring; one went out on disability; another was promoted to a different division; another went to another company and so on. When I originally signed the account, I was told Coca-Cola would use Private Eyes forever if we did a good job. We had successfully serviced them for all of their background checks, drug screens, physicals, MVR's and Driver Qualification File Maintenance. In fact, Coca-Cola now represented 85 percent of Private Eyes' revenue.

Another issue posing a problem came from my vendor for drug screening. A larger company bought the vendor, and Coca-Cola was no longer the most important client there. They stopped providing the same level of service, which was upsetting to both Coca-Cola and me.

What made the whole year a trifecta was the new employee at Coca-Cola who was newly in charge of the screening program. She started a new RFP process, which was expected, and Private Eyes was a finalist in the process, which was also expected because the current HR team loved working with us. However, sometimes, a new person wants to make their imprint on the job, so they change all the vendors. And that's what happened.

It was a dark day when Coca-Cola called me in late 2007 to let me know the company would be transitioning away from Private Eyes in the next year. Five women called me on a conference line to give me the news and reassure me I would be alright. I got in my car, drove to a parking lot down the street and cried.

How could I replace 85 percent of my revenue before I ran out of money? There were so many people depending on me, from my employees to the landlord, my mortgage, the bank, my sons…I felt the weight of the world on my shoulders. I cried harder.

Finally, I called my friend John, who came to the parking lot and tried to calm me down in my car. John reminded me that God was the CEO of Private Eyes, and I could depend on God for ideas to replace Coca-Cola. That reminder allowed me to finally quit crying and feel a little calmer.

Next, I had to tell my team of 75 people.

I didn't tell them right away. I didn't have the words; I didn't have a plan; and I didn't have the courage. It would take a while for Coca-Cola to do the transition, so I had some time to come up with what to say and do.

At a women's business conference, I met another CEO and confessed to her what was happening.

"Just start over," she said. "Scale back to your million-dollar company and rebuild. Why are you taking it so personally?"

Not to sound like Meg Ryan in *You've Got Mail*, but shouldn't business be personal? Private Eyes had always felt personal to me, and we prided ourselves in giving highly personalized service. Instead of taking her advice, I gathered the team and told them Coca-Cola would be leaving. There was complete silence as employees processed the information.

I promised them there would be life after Coca-Cola, although I wasn't completely sure of that myself. Private Eyes pivoted quickly and started marketing to other companies, but it turns out sometimes things get worse before they get better.

In 2008, Coca-Cola Enterprises transitioned out and away from Private Eyes and the financial crisis hit the United States in October. At that point, I started to think I was a shit magnet, and that God was punishing me for something. Of course, I was so wrapped up in my own misery, I couldn't see that I was personalizing a nationwide financial crisis!

We had received RFPs from other large companies, and I was hoping those might replace Coca-Cola. We had just won the RFP from Limited Brands, but the economy butchered that business, and the RFP was canceled.

Trying to save as many jobs as possible, I didn't cut back on staff or space soon enough, and eventually, all of my personal savings were invested in Private Eyes. I was headed to bankruptcy, and I was terrified.

I contacted my friend, Tracey Hirt, Founder of RPM Mortgage, and asked her if she knew a bankruptcy attorney.

"I do, but you are not going to be a loser and quit and give up like the rest of these assholes," she replied. "You are going to teach everyone you know how to do background checks and start selling and work harder and keep going."

Her pep talk was appreciated, but I did get the name of a bankruptcy attorney. I decided it would be wise to have a Plan B. I explained to the attorney that I had an SBA loan attached to my home, where I lived with my boys, and that was maxed out for $250,000.

"Where will you move with your kids?" he asked. "Do you have money for first and last month deposits?"

I didn't. I barely had money for groceries.

My back was against the wall. I had to do what Tracey said -- get back to work and make it happen so I could keep the house and support my boys. I didn't want to; this was the most painful, fearful time I had ever experienced around money. When I was jobless, penniless and living on the street in Phoenix, it wasn't good, but I didn't have other lives depending on me back then.

At this point, it felt like the weight of the world was on my shoulders and I wasn't feeling up to the task. I crawled into bed and pulled a big blanket over me, thinking, I'm done.

—————◄►—————

Get Out of Bed

"Sandra, you have to get out of bed and go into the office."

Martín had never seen me like this – hell, *I* had never seen me like this! He crawled under the blanket with me. He wrapped his arms around me.

"I will help you. We can do it."

Martín's words were comforting, and I knew he was right. I couldn't stay under that blanket forever and I had to get out of bed. I got dressed and Martín met me at the door with a hot tea. We drove to the office and once I walked through the door, my energy kicked in.

Martín immediately started working the phones with telemarketing. "No one is responding," he called out from his office.

"Keep calling!" I shouted back.

My telephone line rang, and it was a woman from Astra (now WBEC-Pacific) the regional partner organization (RPO) for Women's Business Enterprise National Council (WBENC). I was a member of the organization and had benefitted greatly from my association with the group. The call was to let me know that I had been selected as the WBE Star for our RPO and that they would be sending me to Baltimore, MD in March of 2009 to the celebration for the national organization.

"I guess we will still be here next year because you have an appointment," exclaimed Nenita, one of my long-time employees and manager.

Martín said he was switching from the telemarketing campaign to starting an email marketing campaign. I knew nothing about email campaigns at the time, but I welcomed any new ideas and Martín's enthusiasm.

Another employee pulled me aside and said, "You're going to depend on this guy for marketing? He doesn't even know what a CFO is!" I told him we were trying everything, and he should think of a way he could contribute to bringing in some new business.

Martín's email campaign began, and appointments started trickling in. Soon, we had appointments scheduled all day from 6am-6pm doing sales calls and demos.

From 2009-2010 Private Eyes grew 100 percent and started to pay off the company debt. From there we grew about 30 percent each year for the next few years. Every year that we had growth we started to increase profit and decrease debt until the entire debt was paid off. Our emergency marketing campaign, which included email, phone, events, and referrals, all worked together to replace our largest client.

Never again did I allow one client to be the source for 85 percent of our revenue after that experience. I also learned we could streamline personnel and office space to make Private Eyes more profitable and secure.

Drunk with Love

Once Martín and I became engaged to be married, neither of us wanted to wait to make it legal. I knew I didn't want another big wedding, so when Martín suggested we go to Las Vegas over the Memorial Day weekend 2010 and get married there, I said yes again. The boys were scheduled to be with their father for the weekend, so we were free to go.

I went shopping for a wedding dress and wound up in a small boutique. The owner of the shop was helping me but didn't know the occasion for the dress. I spied a beautiful red dress with spaghetti straps that was not what I had in mind for a wedding dress. The dress fit like a glove and was just gorgeous. As I examined how it looked on me in the mirror, I explained the occasion to the shop owner and my hesitation to buying it.

"If not now, when?" she asked. Sold.

Martín wore a suit with a red tie. He looked great! We went to the Valley of Fire in the desert and got married at sunset. It was very romantic.

"Will you take this man to be your lawfully wedded husband?" asked the man officiating the vows.

"Sure!" I shouted.

Martín and I were so giddy with happiness and my enthusiastic response to the question took us both by surprise. We started laughing and couldn't stop. We barely made it through the rest of the vows because we couldn't quit giggling. From the outside, we probably looked like we were drunk, but I was celebrating 22 years of sobriety that year. We were drunk with love. I always slept on Martín's chest and fell asleep hearing his heartbeat. He has brought me a calmness and comfort that has always made me feel safe. Who wouldn't want that forever?

I arrived at work on Monday morning with a love hangover, smiling from ear to ear. Leave it to Steve to try to burst my happiness bubble. He called me almost the moment I arrived in the office.

"I heard you got married," he started.

"No, I did not," I lied. I was irritated that I felt the need to lie; Martín's and my weekend was so beautiful and precious to me, and I didn't want Steve poking around in it. We had been divorced for six years and my weekends were none of his business.

"I pulled your marriage license," he replied.

Now, I was angry. "*Why*???" I snapped at his sneakiness.

Steve recognized the anger in my voice, and perhaps even regretted the intrusion into my life. After all, he and his girlfriend had made it very clear to me that their life was no business of mine. He pivoted in his approach.

"When are you going to tell the boys?" he asked.

Nothing was changing in our household; Martín had been taking care of us for several years already and the boys were used to him being around – even depended on him in many ways. Martín and I had originally decided that next year we would have a celebration in our backyard on Memorial Day weekend and that would be when we celebrate every year. That would give us time for the boys to get used to the idea of Martín as their stepdad.

"Please don't say anything to the boys," I said. "I will tell them." He reluctantly agreed.

With our secret out, I didn't completely trust Steve or his girlfriend to not slip up and spill the beans. So, Martín and I decided to have a real ceremony with the boys on the beach on July 4, 2010. I planned a beach getaway in Parajo Dunes, California, and the only people invited were the boys and my friend, John, who would officiate the vows for us. Two of Martín's cousins came as witnesses for us. I found a house on the beach and rented it for a month.

We told the boys we were taking a month-long vacation at the beach and while we are there, we were going to have a wedding. Cole was very upset.

"But I wanted you and dad to get back together," he cried. I recalled the conversation he and I had on the kitchen floor one night when he confessed that he didn't think his dad was going to be ok.

"That is normal to feel that way son, but your dad and I will never get back together, Cole," I said. "We both love you and Adam; that will never change. And your dad will be ok."

"But mom," he argued. "You said you would never get married again!"

"I know," I said, wrapping my arms around him. "And I cannot believe I want to again!"

"What if it doesn't work out with you and Martín and you get divorced again?" he asked.

"Well, Cole, there are no guarantees in life," I replied. "But I love Martín and I think we make a good team, so I am willing to try it again."

I finished the conversation with a description of the house on the beach and told them we wanted them to go with us and celebrate and stay for a honeymoon with us on the beach. The idea of a month on the beach overshadowed any other objections either of them had. Delighted, they agreed to go.

Then, Steve called me.

"I heard you rented a place on the beach for a month," he said. "And there's going to be a wedding?"

Who is the mole that is feeding Steve my personal information?

"Yes," I said. "But you are not invited."

Steve laughed. "How about if I come stay there with the boys for a week afterwards."

Was Steve really asking me to cut my honeymoon short so he and his current girlfriend could swoop in and enjoy the vacation I had planned with the boys? I couldn't believe the balls on this guy…

It is a testament to how potent being drunk on love can be that I agreed to the idea. Being generous and taking the high road could not hurt me, I reasoned, and I knew the boys would enjoy being with their dad.

"Okay, you can have the house for a week," I acquiesced. "Just write me a check for a couple hundred dollars and we'll let you have it."

"Why?" he asked. "You already paid for it."

"If you can find a place on the beach for a week for less, go get it," I replied, calmly. "But if you want to use this one, you can pay me a couple hundred."

He agreed with no more argument. Smh!

So, after we had spent a couple of weeks at the beach with the boys and tied the knot in both English and Spanish, we left. Then, Steve and his girlfriend came and stayed with the boys.

Martín and I drove back home, still drunk in love.

———•◦———

Stay in Your Lane

The wedding didn't change anything except the jewelry we wore on our left hands. We kept our same routine and responsibilities. If the boys felt a difference, they never mentioned it. Martín started spending more time at the office and I was grateful, but we hadn't found the perfect niche for him yet.

One Friday, Martín said he had a surprise for me, and we would have to leave the office right at closing.

"OK, but before we go, I want to go to Left Bank for a burger," I said.

"Then you have to leave work early," he replied. "So, we will have enough time."

I rarely left the office early; I was conscientious of how cutting out early looked to employees. When I didn't leave on time, Martín was annoyed.

"We are not stopping at Left Bank for a burger," he said. "We have to get on the road."

When I am hungry, it's not wise to deny me food. I became hangry at him…really hangry. He tried stopping at a several fast-food places where we could take our burgers with us.

"I don't eat fast food," I said, somewhat bitchy. Martín just stared straight ahead and kept driving, probably listing in his head the number of times we had eaten fast food in the last month, but he was too wise to mention it.

When we arrived at the bed and breakfast, it was pouring down rain, which didn't help my mood. Once inside, we were warmly greeted by the couple who owned the B&B, and my hanger started to melt. After signing in, we were shown to our room, which was beautiful. There was a crackling fire going on in the fireplace, the big bed was turned down for the evening, and everything about the room was inviting.

The owners were very gracious and made us feel so welcome. By now, Martín was also hungry, so we went back out into the rain to try a restaurant the B&B owners recommended. This time, though, the rain seemed *romantic*, rather than a hassle.

The morning was half over before I opened my eyes. I couldn't believe how long I slept. The bed, the fire, the room…it was all so cozy, I didn't want to move. By the time we went downstairs to breakfast, all the other guests had eaten and left. Since they had no other guests, the couple sat down at the dining table and talked with us. It was a conversation we definitely needed to hear.

We asked the couple how they got along working together. They explained that they had both retired from corporate America and always wanted to have a B&B. They had an honest conversation about what each person was really good at doing. Once that was established, they went about their daily tasks and stayed in their lane. Each person could ask for help, but if they didn't ask, the other let them do it their way.

"That agreement allowed us to work well together," said the wife.

"And stay happily married," added the husband.

Martín and I loved hearing how they worked together. It reminded us of our own agreements we had made, and we decided to add that couple's agreement to our short list. We were aware that we were already doing it, but we now have it as an established agreement.

On the drive back home, we talked about the areas of Private Eyes that Martín had enjoyed working on, where he thought he could bring improvement and what I felt was needed. It was a great discussion, and our working together became even more fun and productive.

That was one of the best surprise weekends ever. It was very romantic, and it deepened our understanding of each other and the life we were building together. I am so grateful we didn't stop for a burger on the way!

Working Smarter; Not Harder

With Private Eyes back on track by 2010, we were a much leaner machine. We had scaled back on office space, personnel, and the long hours we had been putting in to rebuild. We also invested with our software vendor to build a quicker, more efficient program. As we continued to come up with ways to solve our clients' challenges, we were presented with a new one.

Tracey, the friend who told me I couldn't quit after Coca-Cola left, called me with an idea.

"A new rule has been implemented that requires us to get a 4506 Transcript to verify borrowers' income from the IRS for mortgage loans," she said. "The service costs us $25-$30 per year per transcript. Why don't you start offering this service?"

I loved the idea and figured our background checks software would work perfectly to produce those documents. So, I started 4506-Transcripts. com and Tracey became our first client. However, as my IT guys like to remind me, I need to consult them before making promises to clients – or starting new businesses based on technology I *assumed* would work!

Our launch of 4506-Transcripts.com did not go as smoothly as we would have liked. Private Eyes' software was built for background checks, so while the software worked, it was cumbersome for both my team and the client. In order to fix that problem, I started *another* company to build the website and develop the software to make it user friendly for both my team and the client.

My sister, Diane, was interested in working for the business and she lived in Nevada, so we registered 4506-Transcripts.com in that state. As the economy started rebounding, her original business came back to life and she decided to focus on that, rather than 4506-Transcripts. com. The company was already incorporated in Nevada, so I just left it there. That turned out to be a wise move.

Once we cleared all those hurdles, the 4506-Transcripts.com business took off. Cole Taylor Bank came on board and with it, they brought over 2,000 brokers to us right away. It was a very exciting time, and I am grateful for Tracey's friendship, mentoring, and inspiration.

Over the years, as the company grew, I decided to build on our new software platform that we had developed for 4506-Transcripts.com. We utilized that platform as a base to build on our proprietary software for background checks and stop using a third-party software vendor. The vendor we were using told us in the beginning of our relationship that they would program anything for us; that we could call them anytime; they were here for us. After a while, however, they started telling us we called too much; we needed to start using a trouble ticket; they couldn't program new requests this year, maybe next year, or they wouldn't program our request at all. After years of dealing with the pushback, it was time to work smarter; not harder.

We had started this project in 2019 prior to the pandemic, so once the pandemic hit, I told my team we were going to transition into a marketing company and keep bringing on new clients to get through that time and we were going to put all extra team resources on the software.

We deployed Private Eyes Easy Knowledge Platform (PEEK) at the end of 2020 and moved all our clients over to it. In addition, we created Form4506-C.com website, but all services are offered through Private Eyes Screening Group, the parent company I created to house our screening businesses.

All of these moves proved to be game changers for Private Eyes! The programs were running smoothly, and we were able to service a variety of requests quickly and painlessly.

Sandra Goes to College

In 2012, I was selected to go to the WBENC Tuck Program at Dartmouth College. Sponsored by IBM and WBENC, the one-week program provides tools, networks, and opportunities needed to succeed in business. It's taught by MBA faculty from the Tuck School of Business at Dartmouth. One of my clients sponsored me to go to work on my business instead of in my business. The course changed my life and the steps that I took next.

One of the biggest ah-ha moments came from the professor who taught accounting at Dartmouth. She said, "Girls, if you are smart enough to make it, you are smart enough to invest it. You do not need someone to tell you what to do with it."

I had paid all of the company debt off by this time and had a lot of cash in Private Eyes, which I thought would add more value to the company. She explained that you can always prove the income was made, but that we should take the money out of the company and invest it.

"If you need to, lend it back to the company," she explained. "And pay yourself up to 18% interest."

What a brilliant idea! Interest income is taxed less than W-2 income… where can you get that ROI? She emphasized paying taxes first on the money, then investing the rest in real estate, stocks, another business, rental properties or investment properties. The idea was to create other revenue streams.

"This will protect you if something happens to the company," she said.

Wow. I found myself nodding in agreement. I had seen the unforeseen happen to my businesses and I wanted to protect Private Eyes from ever going through that again.

I went back to Private Eyes with new information and updated my goals. I bought my first rental property in 2012. This learning has given me the tools to grow my net worth tenfold in the last 12 years.

Gratitude for the client who sent me to the Tuck program cannot be measured. And I finally got to college!

Organizations that Changed My Life

There are so many professional organizations and groups offering all kinds of networking. It's hard to know which ones are right for you. I wasn't seeking membership in any organization, but the right organizations found me.

Women's Business Enterprise National Council (WBENC) was the first organization I joined. Actually, the women I worked with at Coca-Cola Enterprises introduced me to the organization and suggested I get certified through it. The certification required that at least 51 percent of the business is owned and managed by women; a woman has contributed capital and/or industry expertise; and has control, and U.S. citizenship established of the majority ownership. I met all the requirements and thought it sounded interesting and maybe I could do some good networking. I found it to be much more than that. I have been so grateful for the introduction to this group of women. The growth I've achieved through working with WBENC has proved invaluable. I have watched this organization grow to over 20,000 women-owned businesses. Pamela Prince-Eason, CEO of WBENC, has done an amazing job as the leader that has moved things forward.

When I was offered a spot in the WBENC Tuck program at Dartmouth College, I wasn't sure what to expect. However, the professors' words of wisdom were embedded in my mind as Martín and I continued to invest in real estate, residential rental properties, a commercial building for the business in Reno, an investment property on the beach, and more. We also added to our stock market portfolio, while continuing to develop the business and our software.

Private Eyes grew into a software company that provides the service of background checks and health screening for employers across the nation plus income verifications and employment verifications for lenders providing SBA and Mortgage loans. Our team has helped people get the jobs and homes of their dreams, and we've made safe workplaces possible.

With two Private Eyes offices operating, there are a lot of spinning plates in the air at any given time. Establishing 4506-Transcripts.com (now Form4506-C.com) in Nevada turned out to be providential.

Setting up an office for 4506-Transcripts.com in Reno did not make life easier, but it made it much better. The commute between our two offices was already longer than three hours; more if there was traffic. But in Reno, we were able to purchase a building and arrange for the company to pay us for renting it, instead of paying someone else. Martin and I bought a house and moved there ourselves in 2013. Six years later, we downsized our leased office in Walnut Creek, California, and brought much of that work to Reno.

A surprising benefit to being in Reno has been our staff retention. We have been able to keep staff for years longer than what we experienced in the San Francisco Bay Area. Also, the growth opportunity at our company is greater in Reno. And that, in itself, has made a huge difference to our culture. We have built a dynamic, loyal, and passionate team that is committed to providing great service. Like most companies since the pandemic, we now have a hybrid model for our employees and have been able to add talent in various locations.

In 2016, my Operations Manager, Nenita, left unexpectedly. It was a big loss for Private Eyes; she had been with the company for many years. I was trying different things to get the right person to help me run the operation, but nothing was clicking.

At the end of the year, I still had no operations manager, and I was invited to a meeting of Vistage Worldwide. Vistage Worldwide is a peer group for CEO's and business owners. Reluctantly, I went to the meeting. They asked if they could process my operations manager issue. Not knowing exactly what that entailed, but figuring I couldn't lose anything by saying okay, I said yes. I told them what I had tried and the unsatisfying outcomes. It was interesting to listen to their process to help me solve my problem.

"There is one team member, Frank, who has been working with me for over a decade on the management team," I interjected. "I do confide in him often."

After hearing more about Frank, they told me I should ask him if he wanted to become a Director of Operations.

I went back to the office and talked to him the same day. We talked about what was needed most in the company at that time and I asked if he would be interested in doing that work. He jumped at the opportunity.

"What title do you want?" I asked.

"Director of Operations!" he responded. Perfect!

This was another decision that changed my life. Frank upped the game for Private Eyes. He worked out great with the team, who was enthusiastic about his promotion. Our retention rate improved, as well as our culture. He was critical to all areas of improvement internally and keeping our clients satisfied for the next seven years. He retired at the end of 2023. One year later, he has just returned to do some consulting work with us. Relationships matter with clients and the team; you just never know what will happen next.

I am still a member of Vistage as the group has helped me to become a better leader and work through any issues that arise. My current Chair, Darrell Jackson has grown our group from four members when he started with us to 18 members. We are running companies from 1 million in revenue to 500 million in revenue, so we can support each other as a board for each company and help when we need to discuss any area of our business or life. It works. I am grateful to my group and to Darrell. While we have a lot of spinning plates in the air at Private Eyes, many of them are now on autopilot. We are all busy, but not overworked, we are all challenged, but not stressed out and we are enjoying the fruits of our labor. I give credit to the professional organizations I joined and the wonderful people I've met through them.

Success

When I think back at all the crazy, million-dollar ideas I kept presenting to my dad when I was younger, it seems obvious that I was an entrepreneur just waiting for the right idea to come along. But I believe my willingness to make necessary changes in my life, learn from others, stand up for myself, take risks, and do what's on my plate, has been key to my success.

During the times I only had scraps of faith, I leaned on a strong determination and persistence that sometimes surprised even me. Being told I couldn't do something only made me want to prove I could, and when the numbers were stacked against me, my natural inclination was to keep going until I was on top of them. Even when I was under my blanket after losing the Coca-Cola account, determination and persistence were peeking under the cover, just waiting for me to come out.

All my life experiences – good and bad – have taught me invaluable lessons. The people who have supported me through addictions, bad choices, building two multimillion-dollar companies, parenting, death, two marriages, and near bankruptcy, have nourished my hunger for information, education, and spiritual and physical support. *They have taught me to think differently.*

I am a different leader today than I was 35 years ago. I am calmer under stress; I know things will work out; I have other CEO friends whom I can call upon; and now, I always use my inside voice when problems arise!

The leadership courses and mentoring I've received have also seeped into my personal life. I am a different wife, mother, friend, and mentor. I've walked into the woods of fear and despair and come out on the other side so many times that I can offer sound advice; I can be there for someone who needs a listening ear or a shoulder to cry on; I am openly grateful for every opportunity and every word of mentoring shared with me.

Remember when I called myself Sandy Luck Luck, because I thought I was a lucky girl? I don't call it luck anymore. I worked too hard for my success to think it was just luck. Success came through a combination of many qualities that I had to develop and build upon, some more easily than others.

The final key ingredient to my success, I believe, is to acknowledge providence in my life. Mahatma Gandhi said, "Providence has its appointed hour for everything. We cannot command results; we can only strive."

Striving, which includes all the aforementioned is what we're all doing in hopes providence will kick in. I have experienced it too many times in my business and personal life to disregard it. And I am so grateful for it. Understanding that providence plays a big role in my life makes me enthusiastic about what may develop next and who we may work with next. It helps keep me calm when weathering storms and makes me look forward to the wonderful things that are in store!

My grandma always wanted to live to be 100 years old and she did, and she used to say, "I cannot wait to see what happens next!" I think

I have her genes and I know why she always said that. I cannot wait to see what happens next!

Acknowledgments

I once heard that great things never come from our comfort zones. The people who have helped me get out of my comfort zones (or discomfort zones, as I look back on them) are many. I have such a deep sense of gratitude for everyone who has prodded me, swore at me, and has been generous with their time, and lent a listening ear, advice and even money, to propel me forward to a life of success. All have been important to me, so I am listing everyone alphabetically…

Angela Blodgett is one of my favorite mom-friends, we supported each other when her two girls and the boys were young. We still laugh today about her inviting me to go to the zoo with the kids. I started work at 5am and left at 10am to pick up Cole to go to the zoo in Oakland. I was trying to be great at work and as a mom. When we all stopped for snack time, Cole was the only one who had a mom forget to bring anything. Angela, said, "I got it, I brought Cole snacks." We still laugh about this today. She was always a supportive super mom friend and a great hairdresser.

Maria Castellon, owner of Bench-Tek, my friend came from Mexico and did not know English when she first started working in the U.S. as a Janitor for IBM. Through educational programs including Latino Entrepreneurial Program now she owns a multimillion-dollar manufacturing company in Silicon Valley, CA.

Margaret Chiavini has been very inspirational to me for more than 30 years. She worked for Steve and kept in touch with me after our divorce. She is my younger son's godmother and one of the most gracious and supportive people I know. She lives a life of optimism and gratitude. Margaret and her husband, Paul, have been great friends, even inviting us to go in on a vacation condo together for $200 a month. At the time, we couldn't afford it! Thankfully, things changed.

Madeline Connor is my friend who is a massage therapist and went with the boys and me to Nebraska two weeks before my dad died. She was a single woman who did not have kids and had traveled to Korea and Thailand to become an expert at her trade. She has always been a girl of the world. She still gives me massages all these years later. She is a massage therapist and a therapist who lets me vent on the table. She is a master at her trade and taught me that taking care of your physical self with massages, meditation, working out, walking, and yoga is part of staying healthy and becoming a great leader. I have more stamina, optimism, and positive energy for building my great life when I take care of myself first. Then, I can take care of others.

My husband Martín Del Carmen taught me what true love looks and feels like. His first concern has always been for my boys and me. His quiet self-confidence and sense of identity has made my dream of building an empire possible. Martín is a strong pillar that I lean on in every aspect of my life. I will always be grateful to him for getting me out of bed and back into the office when I was at my lowest point. Then, watching him take charge of an email marketing campaign to help get us back on our feet when our office staff was still in a daze, motivated everyone. Anything is possible to Martín, and I admire his strength, integrity, and loving way he has taken care of my boys and me. He inspires and supports me every day so we can live our best life, making me laugh along the way. Thank you, Martín, for choosing to go on this journey with me!

I also want to thank all my family on Martin's side. Without all their support and help we would not be where we are today. They say it takes a village, and it is a blessing to know that I have all his cousins on our team. I love you all and the gift of growing my immediate family. You have made a difference for Cole and Adam and the men they have become.

Karen Gladstone, we have been friends since I started my first business. When I was in Phoenix, she would call me at night and ask me to come to spend the night because she was scared in her big house with her two-year-old. She would lure me with a promise to make me a bacon, lettuce, and tomato sandwich – my favorite -- if I came over. So, I always would. I lived down the street at the time in a one-bedroom apartment. We are still good friends today and no matter how much time passes, we are connected. She told me I just had to have kids as it was the best. She has been a rock star in the mortgage insurance business the entire time I have known her and has many awards for top sales in the US.

Kerry Gross for inviting me to go on my first adventure out of Nebraska, and then lending me $10,000 to buy dairy cattle. Without his support at that time, I might not have been able to do my first business with cattle and move to Arizona.

Dee Hays, owner of Excellence in Engineering, is my go-to person to talk me off the ledge. She owns a couple of businesses now and I return the favor whenever it's needed. We met years ago at a C200 protégé program. She is a "scratch sister," a self-made, successful female business owner I am fortunate to have in my life.

Tracey Hirt is a powerhouse, a mentor, and a dear friend. Whenever we got together, I always learned something from her. By watching her, I learned how to move from having a lifestyle business to having a business that created generational wealth.

Sandy Hunter, owner HunterHawk. In 2008, when I was afraid and heading to bankruptcy, Sandy Hunter, owner of HunterHawk, met me at Applebee's for lunch. I was teary and feeling defeated. Sandy said, "Baby girl, my business is doing great. If you need $100,000, I will give it to you. You are going to be ok." By offering me money, her confidence in me was overwhelming and just what I needed to hear to keep going. I didn't take her up on the offer, but I was so grateful for the confidence she had in me.

Arlene Inch, Chairwoman of TransPak, is the woman who taught me the more you give the more you get. She has invited Martín and me to all kinds of philanthropic events, like Jane Seymour's Open Hearts Foundation. She has had her business for 50 years and has grown it to over $500 million. I truly admire her and am grateful for her friendship. I love the time we share, walking, eating and attending events. She taught me that whatever happens, just deal with it quickly and move on!

Craig Johnson for giving me the opportunity to sell and manage Mortgage Information Services and later lending me $10,000 to start RMCR.

Robyn Kloner started off as a client at RMCR. She is a top mortgage loan officer in Phoenix. She quickly became a friend given our mutual Midwest upbringings and our subsequent move to Phoenix to become successful in the mortgage industry. When I was pregnant with Cole, she was pregnant with her son, Andrew. Knowing I needed support at home, Robyn gave up her nanny, Becky to help me through those first few months. Becky was an amazing gift to my family during that time.

Mary Martin and I met at a wedding in Phoenix and became instant friends. We shopped together and spent time together; we were pregnant at the same time. She is a super mom and raised four beautiful successful children. She is one of the happiest, most beautiful people that I know. I admire her strength and determination to be a mother and wife. She has provided a listening ear, given parenting tips and just been a great friend.

Olsa Martini is another friend who I have learned so much from. She came to the U.S. from Albania; she did not know how to speak English, yet she started her Engineering and Professional Staffing Services in 1996, Olsa Resources. She is an amazing woman, mother, and business owner, and she taught me the ropes to navigate WBENC. We have tons of laughs and great food when we are together.

Noel Murphy is my neighbor in Danville, California. She was an assistant teacher at the grade school the boys attended and taught them both in 4th grade. When her husband passed about 15 years ago, we started inviting her to dinner whenever we were home. She was with us a lot from then on and it was great for the boys. They respected her and were always nice to her. She could get them to talk about anything, even when they were teenagers. When Adam was confirmed in the Catholic Church, he asked her to be his sponsor. She has been a huge gift to us—our adopted grandma—and we consider her part of our family.

John Qualtrough is a former Air Force Chaplin, whom I could call between 5am-9pm seven days a week and he would always take my call. He offered encouragement and always told me "You've got this." He would listen to me and pray for me, and I am grateful for his help.

Becky Robbins has already been mentioned in this book, but I wanted to make sure she was on my gratitude list because she is an amazing coach, friend, and mentor. She introduced me to Landmark Worldwide and Phoenix Youth at Risk, both of which changed my life. She helped me to believe I could move mountains and if I couldn't, then the right person that I would hire could.

Melissa Simons is the founder of *Diversity Professional Magazine*. Over the years I have known her, I've watched her grow her business, buy her first home, and become financially strong. She has made me a cover girl twice by putting me on the cover of *Minority Business Entrepreneur* magazine and *Diversity Professional* magazine. The cover of this book is one of the photos from the last photo shoot we did together.

Aaron Spaulding was a Youth at Risk who I partnered with when he was 13 years old in Phoenix, Arizona. I have stayed his committed partner for the last 35 years and watched him accomplish his dreams including 22 years in the U.S. Navy, becoming a great husband and father, and now on to his second career transitioning from the military to civilian life. I could not be more proud of all he is done. It has been a special gift to watch Aaron grow into the amazing man that he has become.

Tiffany Stuart, owner of Dynamic Office and Accounting Solutions is a resilient, self-made success story herself. Our kids would swim together on weekends when they were little. She got divorced the same time I did, and we both have had our own businesses. We have always supported each other as single mothers, businesswomen, relationships, etc. She is a scratch sister. I admire her strength, love her roasted chicken, and am grateful for her support and friendship.

DeeDee Towery, retired owner, ProActive Business Solutions. DeeDee and I became friends after meeting at the 100 Top San Francisco Bay Area Women-Owned Business List events around 2004. She and I clicked on many levels, and she supported me with my business and my relationship with Martín when we first got together. She is a dear friend, another scratch sister, and we gave each other confidence when we needed it.

I am also grateful to my sisters and brothers – Wyatt Deines (deceased), Tanya Prickett, Annette Henkel, Elaine Eberhardt, Diane Deines, Clayton Deines, Janel Hendricks, and Duke Deines – for reminding me of events from our childhood and correcting my foggy memory, for being sounding boards throughout our lives and being forgiving whenever I was having a drama. I love you all.

Book Group Questions

1. Did you find this book inspiring and/or motivating?

2. How did this book relate to your own life experiences or interests?

3. Did this book inspire you to take any action or make any changes in your life?

4. What was the most useful idea you learned from this book?

5. What would you like to learn more about after reading this book?

6. How credible and relatable were Sandra's life experiences?

7. Who have been the positive and/or negative influences in your life? Explain how.

8. Have you ever owned a business that failed? How did you deal with it?

9. Have you ever dealt with addictions in your life?

10. Have you ever been in a toxic romantic relationship? If so, how did you get out of it?

11. Would you recommend this book to someone? Why or why not (or with what caveats)?

12. What kind of reader would most enjoy his book?

13. How much did you know about this book before picking it up?

14. What surprised you the most about the book?

15. Did the book change your opinion about anything, or did you learn something new from it? If so, what?

16. Did it evoke any emotions? Make you laugh, cry, or cringe?

17. What do you think were the major events or challenges that shaped Sandra's life?

18. How did Landmark Worldwide change Sandra's life?

19. Did you highlight or bookmark any passages from the book?

20. Do you have a favorite quote or quotes?

21. What were some of your favorite scenes from the book? Why did they stand out to you?

22. Did Sandra succeed in explaining her life story and perspective?

———◆◆———

Printed in Great Britain
by Amazon